other books by this author:

Political Ecosystems

Double Helix Hubris

Visionary Plant Consciousness

Delusions of Normality

Animal Encounters

Animal Encounters

J.P. Harpignies

Cool Grove Press
Brooklyn, New York

copyright © 2014 J. P. Harpignies

all rights reserved under the International and
Pan-American copyright conventions.
Published in the United States by
Cool Grove Press, an imprint of
Cool Grove Publishing, inc., New York.
512 Argyle Road, Brooklyn, NY 11218
http://www.coolgrove.com

All inquiries to info@coolgrove.com

ISBN 10: 1-887276-76-9

ISBN 13: 978-1-887276-68-8

cover design: Tej Hazarika

Printed in the United States of America

*To Linda Miller
and
the Harbin Hot Springs Bookstore*

Contents

Introduction .. 1

Snakes
The Viper on the Path ... 3
The Snakes Under the House 9
Snake Visions: The Cobra and Other
 Archetypal Serpents .. 13

Ungulates
Deer.. 31
The Big Elk .. 33
The Mysterious Cow .. 36

Equines ... 43

Aquatic Mammals
The Seal .. 49
Otters .. 52

Bears .. 55

Rodents
Mice, Rats, Rabbits, etc. .. 65
Squirrels ... 67
Porcupines ... 71

Birds ... 77

Felines
The Pregnant Mountain Lion in the Dark 85
The Cannabis-Loving Kitten .. 88

Women and Cats
1. The Vengeful Siamese Cat .. 94
2. The Psychic Cats ... 97
3. The Death Throes of my Girlfriend's Cat 99

Canids
Coyotes .. 104
Dogs .. 110
The Feral Dog on my Landing 117
Panda ... 121

Primates
Homo Sapiens sapiens .. 126
The Flute Player ... 128
The Perfect Couple ... 132

About the Author ... 141

Introduction

Introduction

I am predominantly an urban creature. I have done a fair amount of hiking and backpacking in mountains, forests and deserts over the years, but I was born in and have lived the lion's share of my life in New York City, one of the world's biggest and densest megalopolises. And yet, as I recently looked back at my life, I was struck by the fact that I've had quite a few deeply affecting experiences that involved animals, both in the city and in the "wild." Some of these were terrifying, some edifying, some humiliating, some joyous, and some tragic, but quite a few were memorable enough that I remember them vividly many decades later.

I suspect that I am not at all exceptional in this regard, and that if most people thought about it, they too would remember a number of interesting incidents in their lives involving animals. If anything I have probably had fewer interactions with animals than most people, as I have never owned a pet of any kind, nor, though I certainly find many animals interesting and feel empathy with animals' suffering, have I ever thought of defining myself as an "animal lover." I certainly have had far fewer dealings with animals than any farmers or rural dwellers, or people who fish or hunt or ride horses or breed dogs or engage in birding or wildlife photography. I've never even owned a camera.

Animal Encounters

So, though at least a small handful of the incidents and some of the perspectives I describe in this text are admittedly a bit out of the ordinary, I did not write this book because I view myself as someone who has had particularly extraordinary experiences with animals. I don't really know why it happened, but for some reason I began remembering these episodes and thinking about them, and more memories kept coming up, so I began to write down my recollections of those animal encounters that felt most significant to me, framing these incidents in the context of specific periods and themes of my life, and this small tome is a collection of a number of those anecdotes.

I think it's likely, surprisingly perhaps given the rapid urbanization of the planet and how separated, both physically and culturally, nearly all modern humans feel from the natural world, that almost all of us could do the same and find that we have had far more interactions with animals than we suspect, and that at least some of those episodes may have some interesting things to tell us about the world and about ourselves.

Snakes

The Viper on the Path

At the age of six I spent one school year living with a family that owned and operated a hotel on a steep hillside overlooking the town of Montreux, on Lac Léman (aka Lake Geneva), in Switzerland (many decades before the jazz festival made the town more internationally known).

My mother, I was told, required some sort of surgery and needed a long convalescence and my father had a work assignment that precluded his taking care of me that year. I, of course, have no idea if this was all strictly true or if there were other family dynamics at play, but at that age one obviously has little understanding of the adult world and no choice but to go along with the program.

I knew the hotel and its owners because my family vacationed there every other year for a few weeks. Also one of my (15 years older, twin) sisters had just married a Swiss man and she lived with him an hour or so away in Lausanne, so at the time our family had ties to that part of Switzerland. I liked the big Cima clan, who were a mix of German and Italian Swiss stock, very kind, hardworking and unpretentious folks, and the hotel was a nice old elegant sort of mini castle with a big tower

and turret and stunning views of the lake below and the mountains in France on the far shore. It directly overlooked the Chateau de Chillon, a small lakeside castle that appears in both Henry James' novella *Daisy Miller*, published in 1878, and more famously in Lord Byron's 1816 poem, *The Prisoner of Chillon*, which is about an unlucky political figure who was imprisoned there in the 1500s. Rumor has it Byron carved his name on a pillar of the chateau's dungeon. Anyway, from the hotel's balconies and lovely decks one could watch hawks circle and glide and swoop down toward their prey below. Among the hotel's patrons were a number of elegant elderly English ladies with their somewhat less old traveling assistants-companions who all sipped tea on the terrace overlooking the Chateau, and a few noisier large French and Italian families.

I helped out in the hotel doing what small chores I could at that age, and I became a little Swiss schoolboy with leather shorts and a knapsack covered in some sort of animal fur. My commute to school involved walking down (or racing if I was running late) a path of some 75 yards to take a tiny funicular, which only ran from the hotel's stop (and upper terminus) down the steep slope to Territet, a small neighborhood just up from Montreux, where I was enrolled in the equivalent of second grade in the public school. The funicular ride took 9 or 10 minutes and made one or two stops in its descent. If I missed my morning funicular, I had to race down very steep trails to get to school on time. The

Snakes

funicular probably couldn't fit more than 8 passengers. In retrospect it's hard to believe it was financially viable, but the two very old men in their railroad conductor garb running it, who punched my funicular pass very formally every morning and afternoon, were undoubtedly retirees supplementing their pensions, and the hotel really needed the service so its patrons could get down to Montreux without always requiring cars or taxis, so I'm guessing it probably lobbied hard to keep the municipality from shuttering it.

My experiences that year were a mix of the nightmarish and the sublime and marked me for life. The first day of school, I got in a pushing match during recess with a kid who insulted me for being American and what seemed like the entire male student body in the courtyard at the time proceeded to beat the crap out of me till I was bleeding fairly profusely. Some even threw rocks. I was the only foreigner in the school and xenophobia is apparently a universal impulse, even among the famously "neutral" Swiss. I think they felt a little bad about it afterwards, and one of the sons of the hotel owner was in one of the classes in the school, at a junior high school equivalent level, and this big, strong lad, appropriately named Urs (i.e. "bear"), was assigned to watch out for me, and I suspect the family had some clout in the neighborhood, so I was left unmolested after that incident. Fortunately I had no major injuries, but it was a terrifying moment, though not nearly as terrifying as what was to follow.

Another scholastic trauma was that I had been taught how to write in block capital letters back in NYC at the UN school in 1st grade, but in Europe they learn script immediately, and I

was way behind and never quite adjusted. To this day my handwriting is an awful, barely legible mishmash of half-formed cursive and capital letters.

The sublime part of the year was that I was taken along on long hikes on the weekends and fell in love with the woods and meadows and gushing torrents and peaks of the Swiss mountains. This early bonding with that terrain led to a life-long love of mountains, which has been a very important feature of my life.

But the most dramatic incident that year involved an encounter with a snake. As I was coming home from school one afternoon, skipping along that path from the funicular stop, a very large viper suddenly appeared in front of me, quite close, blocking my way. It was very agitated and aggressive. I must have surprised it. It seemed immense to me, its silvery, somewhat shiny skin adding to its terrifying otherworldliness. I had been told that one way to differentiate vipers from large local non-venomous snakes was that vipers had a triangular head, and this snake definitely had a triangular head. I screamed almost immediately, and Monsieur Cima, the paterfamilias, came running from the hotel and crushed the viper with a big shovel, cutting off its head in the process. The snake thrashed violently throughout. I don't know how long it all took, though it must have been fast, and I was very lucky that Monsieur Cima was so close by and heard me, as it was a fairly big hotel with large grounds.

My core memory of the actual encounter is vivid. I still shudder as I re-experience the absolute terror I felt. My recollection

of some of the surrounding details is obviously a bit fuzzy, as I'm writing this some 55 years later, but it was one of the most traumatic experiences of my childhood. I had fairly frequent, recurring nightmares involving snakes well into my late twenties, though I'm not sure if those bad dreams were specifically induced by that incident, or if they reflected deeper archetypal fears that would have appeared in my dreams in any event. I strongly suspect that the encounter with the viper at the very least radically heightened and exacerbated those fears and colored those nightmares.

Ten years later my earliest psychedelic experiences also included some terrifying visions of serpents, and throughout my life visions of snakes or serpent-like figures were very frequent whenever I experimented with forays into non-ordinary states of consciousness. Over the years and decades I worked, in meditative, hypnotic and other altered states to get beyond my terror and to psychically integrate the archetypal energies long associated with snakes in many cultures. I definitely haven't lost that fundamental mammalian fear of snakes, but I've also sought to cultivate some reptilian kinesthetic elegance and power in my t'ai chi practice and embrace some of the primordial wisdom that visits our consciousness in the form of serpent imagery. This work with snake visions has become a very important component of my inner psycho-spiritual explorations. I'm not sure if this very early incident helped trigger that lifelong pursuit, but I feel viscerally that the encounter with that viper on that path was somehow a foundational episode in my life.

PS: I hadn't visited that hotel, the Mont-Fleuri, since my teens,

when, some 45 years after that incident and 35 years since I'd last been there, I happened to find myself some 90 minutes away by train, in Geneva, and decided to attempt a Proustian moment by visiting the hotel. The building was still there and hadn't changed much, but Monsieur Cima, I was told, had passed away years before, and it was now an exclusive boarding school for mostly East Asian Muslim girls. The funicular had long stopped running, but the little station and the tracks were still there, rusting, and the path was the same. The whole region all around the lake was far more developed. A major superhighway now lines the lakeshore, radically impacting the view and the experience (the swooshing sound of cars is incessant) as one looks down on the Chateau de Chillon. I suspect there are far fewer vipers around.

Snakes

The Snakes Under the House

Since I hike in wild areas fairly often, I have run into snakes quite a few times in my life subsequent to that early incident, but none of them were frightening. I have of course, inevitably, seen countless garter snakes, which are so common in the Eastern United States, and one summer following a particularly wet spring in the early 1980s, there was a population explosion of the common big black rat snakes such as northern racers and king snakes in the rural upstate hamlet I was renting a house in, and there were hundreds of these dead snakes that had been run over by cars all over the roads. I've never seen that again, though a couple of years after that, a mysterious population spike of squirrels in the region sent thousands of those animals on the march, lemming-like, also onto roads and highways to their demise. Apparently, in the case of the squirrels, that happens every 40 or 50 years and no one knows exactly why.

To get back to the snakes, all the ones I mentioned are non-venomous species, but I have seen a timber rattler or two in the woods in the Catskills (at a sufficient distance not to be worried) and, sadly, those snakes have been relentlessly hunted and are now exceedingly rare in the Northeast. In the Western states, where I have gone on many backpacking trips, I have seen a couple of diamondbacks, and, once, on a solo mountain

expedition near Lake Chelan in eastern Washington State, I had to hike through an area along that lake teeming with rattlesnakes. I had been told to stomp my feet as I walked to alert them to my presence, and it worked: I saw many, but they all slithered away as I approached. I wasn't deeply frightened, but I was hyper alert to my surroundings. There's nothing quite like traversing a poisonous snake-filled landscape to encourage "being here now."

But I had a far more symbiotic, live-and-let-live relationship with a clan of snakes that lived under a house in the Catskills that I spent time in every summer for some twenty years. Some very kind friends would let me use their house during the summers when they lived elsewhere, and in exchange I would watch the place, take care of some repairs and just generally serve as a sort of caretaker, and it turned out that I (and later my then girlfriend and I) were not the house's only inhabitants. We soon discovered that black northern racers lived in the basement and in and around the house's foundation.

In general these housemates were exceedingly discreet. They would mostly remain out of sight. If one of us went to the basement to change a fuse or for some other reason, on occasion we would see one, and sometimes we would spot a pregnant female traveling across the backyard to lay eggs in old woodpiles on the edges of the woods behind the house. They shed their skins in the late summer, and I would find these skins in weird places in the garden or along the sides of the house and collect the most impressively long specimens to show the home's owners, who were, to their credit, comfortable having

these non-venomous snakes as co-occupants. For one thing, these snakes eat rodents, so they must have helped keep the mouse population down, and they eat insects as well. They are also enemies of rattlesnakes, which can be helpful to humans in some instances, but, as I mentioned, there are almost no rattlers left in that region. The racers certainly did no harm, and we grew to like the idea of being able to cohabitate so effortlessly with such a different species.

One late summer, my girlfriend had been away for the weekend with friends and came back in the evening. I was helping her and a friend of hers unload the car, walking in and out of the screen door on the big porch in front of the house, when her friend said to me: "I think one of the homeowners' children must have left a toy snake on the bench on the porch." To my knowledge, these kids did not have such a toy, so I went to look, and there, right in front of the front door, laying on a bench, oblivious to all the people walking by a foot or so away and the repeated slamming of the screen door, was a big, very placid black snake. I had never seen one on the porch before, but it seemed totally unconcerned with all our brouhaha and wasn't moving, and so we went on with our business and left it alone. The next morning I found its skin on the bench. I think these snakes get a bit sluggish in the late summer/early fall and they seek out places with good friction to rub their bodies against to help them get out of their old skins. This bench, with its worn, rugged wood surface, must have been a good skin-shedding spot. The snake may have been totally oblivious to us, but I took it as a sign of trust that it felt comfortable enough to come in a vulnerable state and feel safe right among us, and

to leave its skin literally right in front of our front door.

That was the only time one came so close to being in our living space, and eventually the owners had to sell the house. I had spent some wonderful parts of many summers up there, hiking and meditating among the waterfalls and mountains nearby, listening to the howl of the coyotes, now so plentiful all over the Northeast woods, every night, and meeting some very interesting local people. The cohabitation with those snakes was also an important component of my experience of that place. Feeling their presence under the house, and, undoubtedly anthropomorphically, imagining some sort of mutual respect or symbiotic understanding, subtly changed the daily texture of life there in a way that's hard to articulate.

I really worried that the next set of owners would view them as a threat and get rid of them, but there was nothing I could do to prevent such a situation, as I wasn't involved in the process of selling the place. I hope that clan of northern racers is prospering, and I thank them for tolerating my presence on top of their home for so many seasons.

Snake Visions:

The Cobra and other Archetypal Serpents

Besides my physical encounters with snakes, as I mentioned previously visions of snakes have played an important role in my inner psycho-spiritual life, from the frequent snake-based nightmares that plagued my sleep as a child to far more interesting visions later on, especially during my explorations of the altered states induced by the ingestion of psychedelic plants and drugs. I first took peyote, mescaline, psilocybin mushrooms, and LSD when I was fifteen and sixteen years old (far too young), and almost immediately serpent-related visions factored in to those experiences. In the early disorienting stages of those journeys, as I lay down and closed my eyes, one of the first effects was, as is very common, rapid-fire visual imagery of ever-shifting geometric patterns. Very often this kaleidoscopic onslaught would become an all-encompassing, sinuous wave pattern akin to a portion of a moving serpent's undulating skin, and I suddenly felt as though I, and the whole world, were riding a giant snake. This usually terrified me and I would try to focus my mind elsewhere until this impression passed. It's obviously not an uncommon experience, as exemplified by Jim Morrison's song *Ride the Serpent*.

Animal Encounters

Serpent imagery would return again and again during at least some portions of my (fairly numerous: it was, after all, the 60s and early 70s...) trips, but I always experienced those visions as unsettling or frightening, and it never occurred to me to try to somehow work with or integrate that imagery during those years of excessive youthful experimentation with drugs of all types. I just viewed those episodes as bad portions of my journeys that I had to endure to get to the more ecstatic states. As is so often the case, I left that druggy phase of my life behind by my mid 20s and instead became obsessively focused on physical and psycho-spiritual development, seeking to live a highly disciplined life, which included forsaking all drug-taking, but psychoactive substances re-entered my life some 20 years later in a very different context.

As a side effect of my work, which, among other things, involved editing texts and organizing a wide range of events, many related to environmental issues and many others to psycho-spiritual development, I was introduced to a number of researchers, ethno-botanists, anthropologists, and cultural figures who had explored the serious use of visionary plants in indigenous and other contexts. These were for the most part serious, accomplished, centered people who did really interesting work and whose exploration of consciousness-altering substances was very far from the wild and careless excesses so widespread in my younger days. My curiosity was aroused, and I began a new phase of inner exploration with sacred plants, but using them far less frequently and in a far more measured and contained way than in my youth, and often in the context of organized groups with experienced guides leading the proceedings.

Snakes

This second time around, I did voluminous reading and attended or helped organize many lectures, conferences and colloquia on these matters, and my overall physical, mental and emotional health was far more robust than in my fairly unhinged youth, so I was able to begin working with the material that emerged in these altered states far more productively than I had in my teens and 20s. And serpent imagery returned even more dramatically than it had earlier. I became more and more determined to conquer my fears and desirous to arrive at some sort of deeper understanding of what significance this serpent motif might have in my psyche.

I began reading voraciously about serpent imagery globally, delving into the Naga spirits of India, Chinese dragons, etc., as well as scientific papers (everything from "The Chemical Ecology of Crotaline Snakes" to "The Ecological and Behavioral Context for Pit-Viper Evolution"). Quite often the main snake I encountered in my journeys was some sort of cobra, which was at some moments an actual highly realistic snake and at others a rapidly shifting, radiant being whose body was covered in gleaming precious stones, and which could shape-shift into a plethora of multi-headed, teeming serpents or serpent-like beings. I was surprised to find that this cobra motif was not unique to me. I discovered in a book (*Hallucinogens: A Reader*, edited by Charles Grob) that the famous if controversial "vitamin guru" of the 1950s and 60s, Adelle Davis, who was one of many celebrities (including Cary Grant) who took LSD with the psychotherapist Oscar Janiger in Hollywood in the 1950s, when it was legal and not widely known, had had an acid trip in which a cobra played a central

role. Her journey involved Buddhist and Christian themes, which are not present in my experiences, but the description of the cobra is eerily similar to some of my own visions. Because her cobra seemed clearly linked to Indian and Buddhist imagery, I investigated the serpent lore of India even more intensely, but that reading didn't seem to result in any breakthroughs in my understanding of why this theme was so prevalent in my excursions in modified consciousness.

I came to realize through my reading that serpent visions are extremely common in psychedelic experiences, especially those induced by the Amazonian shamanic brew, ayahuasca, now gaining in global popularity in a rapidly growing underground subculture. A remarkable, seminal text by the Israeli cognitive psychologist Benny Shanon, *The Antipodes of the Mind*, rigorously catalogues the visionary content of ayahuasca experiences of hundreds of people from all sorts of backgrounds, and serpent visions are by far the most frequent animal motif and probably the most common motif, period. Shanon also explores in that book another fascinating theme that reappears surprisingly often in the visions of many individuals from highly diverse backgrounds—ancient Egyptian imagery, even among people who have little or no interest in or knowledge of Pharaonic Egypt. This led me to realize that much of the cobra imagery I tended to see was in fact as much or more Egyptian as it was Indian, and this led me into research on the role of cobras in Egyptian symbolism and mythology and to visits to ancient Egyptian artifact collections in several museums.

During some of my ayahuasca trips the cobra imagery was accompanied by some very odd background narrative ele-

ments. The psychedelic experience generates during some of its stages such a tsunami of images, emotions, and fractured thoughts, memories and plot lines, a bit like an extremely vivid and convoluted dream, that after the trip one can usually only reconstruct a very small percentage, a few fragments of what one has experienced. In my case, one of these murky but recurring sub-plots had to do with snake venoms. I kept seeing images of ancient Egyptian figures concocting alchemical longevity or immortality potions that included cobra venom, and got the sense that these were tightly guarded secrets, and that they were somehow linked to sexual practices or at least internal transmutation of sexual energy into spiritual awakening. Of course this could very well be a complete fantasy. I think it's impossible to know to what extent one's visions in such states are just fanciful, surreal collages our minds generate from bits of cultural flotsam and jetsam, and how much might actually be some sort of "real" information that we pick up (albeit usually in a distorted, hard-to-interpret form) from the collective unconscious or other, mysterious sources.

Because that thematic element kept popping up, though, I started wondering about how I could explore it further. I didn't expect to find some miraculous philosopher's stone or longevity potion, but since this theme recurred so often, I was hoping to find some way to probe it more deeply. I did find some mentions of snake venoms in alchemical formulae in some texts and online, but the sources were mostly in the wildly unhinged new-age esoteric genre, in other words, very far from credible.

It occurred to me that, while I would never try to consume

actual snake venoms, there was one form of these toxins that might be safe enough to experiment with to see if they might trigger interesting insights or dreams: homeopathic remedies. Snake venoms are on rare occasions used in Homeopathy. There are only a small handful of books on the topic, mostly by homeopaths of Indian descent, and, other than the most common snake remedy, Lachesis, usually used for circulatory problems, the very rarely used few dozen other snake venom remedies are available only from a handful of European firms, mostly German. I guess it's not surprising that the few wacky homeopaths willing to travel to the ends of the earth to directly harvest rare snake, spider and other venoms to dilute and test are likely to be German. I read all the texts on the topic I could find and wound up ordering a handful of the remedies of those snake venoms that seemed to correlate most closely to my own psychological make-up.

Let me explain. Homeopathy is a very strange discipline. It is based on a few core principles, one of which is that "like cures like." This means that if one is suffering from a certain set of symptoms, the cure for that condition should be found in the very substance in nature that would cause precisely those symptoms, and a homeopath prescribes that substance to the patient, but in an incredibly highly diluted form, so diluted in fact that there is no measurable chemical trace of the substance. Homeopaths argue that there is a sort of energetic trace of the substance that is obviously very subtle but nonetheless highly efficacious when the right substance has been chosen. To mainstream allopathic medicine, this is viewed as the worst sort of magical thinking. And, indeed,

from a completely secular rationalistic perspective, it is magic. I personally have, not always, but on quite a few occasions had excellent results with homeopathic remedies. If it was nothing but auto-suggestion, it was nonetheless very effective in some instances. I have a lot of respect for the modern scientific method, but I'm capable of entertaining multiple perspectives, even if they're seemingly contradictory. I'm above all a pragmatist, so if magic works, I'll gladly use it…

Homeopathic researchers explore the natural world for potential remedies by looking at the symptoms various plants and other substances cause. So, for example: if a specific snake venom causes blood vessels to rupture in a specific way in victims of bites of that sort of serpent, then that venom might be recommended, again in a radically diluted form, if a patient showed up with that sort of internal bleeding. But, because Homeopathy is also very focused on psychological profiles and uses very complex typologies that include a slew of mental, emotional and spiritual as well as physical factors in classifying patients and prescribing remedies, groups of homeopathic investigators also explore the psycho-spiritual properties of new remedies by consuming them and taking very detailed notes of not only their physical responses but their mental states and dreams and then comparing notes with their colleagues. This is called "testing" a remedy. I read those few accounts of these "testings" involving snake remedies I could find, and ordered a handful of those remedies that most closely matched my own psycho-spiritual profile.

I was still really nervous about taking them, though. I didn't

want to consult a homeopath because I was planning on using these remedies as part of a psycho-spiritual experiment based on visions induced by a controversial drug and not to address an illness, so I didn't think I'd get a very positive response. But I had a former girlfriend, one I had had the longest of all my relationships with, some ten years, but whom I had rarely spoken to in the decade since our fairly sudden and traumatic breakup. We were totally civil on the few occasions we had interacted in the intervening years, and I harbor no ill will whatsoever toward her, but communicating with her is always a tad awkward. The thing is that she is a very gifted acupuncturist and homeopath, and I remembered that she had at one point studied snake venom remedies as part of her training with a very famous homeopath and Jungian psychologist, and very few people on the planet have knowledge of this extremely esoteric niche.

So I overcame my hesitancy and contacted her, and she gave me some initial pointers on how to proceed, but before I could pursue it with her to get more exact data on dosages, etc., Hurricane Sandy destroyed her home and car, so I figured she had much bigger issues to contend with than the strange, drug-addled experiments of an ex, and I didn't follow up. So far, it's been a couple of years, and I have chickened out. I have the remedies in my freezer, but I have been too hesitant to use them. The odds are that nothing much would happen on any level if I took them. There may be nothing measurable in them, but if Homeopathy has any validity whatsoever (a big "if" for skeptics, I know) and can contribute to healing in some cases, then the remedies must also have the capacity to do

Snakes

harm if used improperly. At least, to date, that's been my excuse for my pusillanimity.

A couple of decades ago, during one of my very few uses of pure DMT, the most powerful but short-acting of the psychedelics, I saw a luminescent cobra-like being that then unraveled into what seemed like immense strands of the twisting ladders of DNA, that then also seemed to spin out into highly complex mathematical formulae. This was impressive but also somewhat pointless in that the experience was blindingly short so the symbols I was seeing flashed by so rapidly that I couldn't possible remember them to verify if they might be scientifically cogent or merely just gibberish. Also the vision disappointed me, in that I find the idea that all life might be reducible to mathematical equations fairly depressing.

Still, when I later came across a (then) new book by the anthropologist Jeremy Narby who had done extensive research on shamanism in the Peruvian Amazon, my curiosity was piqued. His book, *The Cosmic Serpent*, deeply explores snake imagery in the visions of Amazonian shamans as well as in global traditional cultures, and finds that the caduceus symbol of intertwined serpents, eerily reminiscent of DNA's structure, is a near universal archetype that seems to emerge from the human unconscious. Given my experiences, this fascinated me. I began to correspond with Jeremy and we eventually became good friends, so when he asked me if I wanted to accompany him on one of his frequent working trips to the Peruvian Amazon (he works for a Swiss non-profit that collaborates closely with indigenous groups to assist them in developing their educational systems and sustainable economic opportuni-

ties) in which we could also participate in shamanic ceremonies involving the ingestion of the famous ayahuasca brew, I agreed. I had taken that potent plant mixture a handful of times, but never in its ancestral home, the jungle environment it has long been used in.

The shaman whose compound we stayed at was someone Jeremy had many years back helped as part of his work supporting indigenous culture, but the fellow had over the years become a sort of rock star among shamans, with European film directors and other glamorous disciples, and I had serious reservations about the scene down there: the shaman's obvious excessive seduction of impressionable young women, the armed guards who patrolled the compound, the shaman's occasional surreptitious use of datura admixtures to his ayahuasca brew (often a sign of "dark" sorcery), etc. But Jeremy did have some influence with the guy, and after a few sessions that were somewhat mild, I asked him to request that I be given a very hefty dose of the strongest brew composed of just the two fundamental ayahuasca components, without admixture plants, and my wish was granted.

I proceeded to have the most explosive serpent visions and sensations I had ever experienced: extraordinary multi-hued snakes slithering through my spine into my brain, exploding my "crown chakra" sending beams of light out the top of my head, etc. The serpent energy seemed to me to be some sort of embodiment of the biosphere, a goddess of Earthly life, but I didn't get a warm and fuzzy feeling. This goddess felt fairly cold and impersonal; she was concerned with the vitality that

undergirds all life, not too much about a mere individual animal, especially a mammal. That said, there was also a lot of intense sexual imagery and sensation thrown in the mix, which involved both a sort of celebration of the teeming fertility of all the species in the jungle environment I was in and in all of nature, as well as wild (and very funny) depictions of my own sexual fantasies. The goddess I was experiencing had an icy, distant vibe, but she also had an intensely erotic one, and a highly comedic side as well. I guess it's not surprising that, since these experiences radically amplify the content of our psyches, they are as filled with paradox as we are.

But to be clear to those who aren't familiar with it: on a strong dose, the ayahuasca experience is hard, often involving some intense disorientation and queeziness, and, for many, especially those not on a rigorous diet, purging. I rarely vomit during these sessions, but I often go through an initial period during which my heart pounds and I feel I could die, and I can't remember who or where I am. One has to let go of the fear of losing one's moorings and of perhaps not being able to regain one's "sanity." One of the reasons to do it is in fact to prepare for death, or at least to learn to let go of one's sense of control. Resisting the ayahuasca is a recipe for a very bad trip. Usually the experience is actually ultimately quite good for the psyche and the body if one is properly prepared, but it can be a grueling ordeal to get through both physically and mentally. My view is that most people probably shouldn't do it.

Because the dose on that occasion was so substantial, I felt totally overwhelmed. Luminescent serpents raced through my

entire body into the center of my skull inducing sorts of brain orgasms and cascades of extraordinarily breathtaking, classic psychedelic visions akin to those captured in the work of such artists as Pablo Amaringo, Alex Grey and Rick Griffin. The sense of possible death was quite strong throughout. It felt to me as though the goddess were saying: "You wanted to see the hidden splendors of nature's mysteries. Well, here are some glimpses, but if your heart stops or you lose your mind in the process, that's not my concern. You're just one puny mammal." I didn't like the shaman whose compound we were staying in, but that experience was the most visually sublime and powerful of all my psychedelic forays, though, as it turned out, it wasn't the most productive.

A few years later I returned to the Amazon and spent a couple of weeks at the retreat center of another shaman, this one of Ashaninka ancestry, in the region of Pucallpa, which is considered the premiere ayahuasca region in the Peruvian Amazon. Jeremy Narby describes it as the equivalent of what Bordeaux is to red wine. This shaman, who Jeremy had also helped in his early days, was a much sweeter and more loveable guy, and it turned out that while I never had any experience as powerful as the one I had on that first visit that I described above, when my time was done after this second visit, I left equipped for the first time with at least a budding sense of how to integrate and use these serpent energies rather than just experience them.

When the group I was traveling with first arrived at his compound, the shaman asked each of us to very briefly explain why we were there and how long we were going to stay. Most

of the folks there had serious physical ailments. That is probably ayahuasca's main function in its native context: people with serious, seemingly intractable or hard-to-diagnose conditions come to it as a last resort when all else fails. A handful were serious apprentices of shamanism who came often to do intensive retreats, including long solitary fasts in the jungle, and a few were spiritual seekers or just curious. I explained to the shaman, Juan Flores, that I had these recurring snake visions and wanted to come to some deeper understanding of what that could be all about. He asked: "Quieres conversar con el serpiente?" And I said: "Si, exactamente." After that initial conversation, before we did any ayahuasca, we all did an initial purge with other Amazonian plants for a couple of days and were given a customized regimen of other herbs to take during our stay, depending on our specific conditions. We then proceeded to take ayahuasca every second night.

For most of my stay my trips were a mix: some were just disorienting, a few felt psychologically productive, but none of them were really memorable. A lot of the shaman's work involves the singing of magical songs, *icaros*, during these ceremonies, and while I enjoyed some of the music in my altered state, I never felt that the songs were affecting me in some psycho-spiritual way, and I never got the sense that the shaman was paying particular attention to me. Juan Flores was around a little bit on occasion but would then disappear completely for a couple of days and would just show up at ceremonies. I liked the guy and, despite the plethora of biting bugs and some disturbing aspects of the scene (the extreme poverty of the locals; nearby oil exploration and clear-cutting; the overhunting of

game in the area; some annoying gringo new agers and conspiracy theorists down there at the same time, etc.), I was appreciating my time down there in this remarkable spot in the jungle alongside a boiling river (like a giant hot spring that extends for miles) with constantly rising steam, but I just got the impression that Juan's work in the ceremonies, while openhearted and authentic, was sort of generic. I didn't really have many conversations with him, but there were people there with terminal cancers, HIV, etc., so I figured they needed attention far more than I did, and I hoped they were getting some. And I kept busy, doing a lot of meditating and reading and t'ai chi, and some jungle hiking (with guides).

A few days before I was slated to leave, Juan Flores showed up one morning at breakfast quite upset, which was unusual. He explained that there had been a misunderstanding or miscommunication with a small group of Americans (two of whom had cancer) who had decided to leave the night before, before what he had planned would be their last ceremony later that night, and that this was very unfortunate. He thought that the healing work he had been able to do with them might hold, but that missing the last ceremony was problematic. I kept my mouth shut, but I didn't understand. Those folks had been there a month and had done some 14 or 15 sessions. What difference could one more make?

The morning of the last day I was going to be there, with one last ayahuasca session to go that night, Juan Flores came up to me and asked: "Are you ready for the last session?" And I, once again a bit baffled by his focus on this "last session" theme, just said that yes, sure, I was. That final session turned out to be

Snakes

totally unlike the first six. It was all about serpent energy. I became part snake, a hybrid being. I felt I wanted to eat a mouse, but I was also still human. The experience wasn't overwhelming. It was sort of a workshop in inner alchemy. I was being shown how to balance my reptilian and mammalian components. I was being shown how to work with serpent-like, sinuous, spiraling energy, both inside my body and in external physical movements, in a very practical, tangible way. This wound up having a profound effect on several aspects of my life, especially on my t'ai chi practice.

I had been working with different forms of that discipline for well over thirty years, but this breakthrough ayahuasca session added a whole new dimension to my understanding of how fundamental "spiraling power" is to t'ai chi and how to begin to embody and express that sort of force. I got a visceral sense of the ancient shamanic origins of many human martial arts in imitating animal movements. This is part of the lore of t'ai chi and some other Chinese martial systems, but feeling it in one's body is very different than understanding it intellectually. This ayahuasca experience radically boosted the value I got from my practice, though, sadly, my aging body can't always physically express my deepened understanding as well as it might have in my younger days. I couldn't help but wish these embodied insights hadn't come to me so late in life, but I was still deeply grateful for these teachings. I also, for the first time, got a lot of images of birds of prey, especially eagles and hawks, and got some inklings of how to tune into and embody some of the "elevated" perspective, ferocity, and single-mindedness of those raptors.

Animal Encounters

During the session Juan Flores came up to me and gave me a wide grin, which he had never done before, and I realized that, while I had been under the impression that he was just generically, somewhat haphazardly leading ceremonies, he had in fact always had an exact sense of everyone there, how long each one of us was going to be staying, and what we were each trying to accomplish. He had, in fact, somehow been working with my energy, lining it all up so that it could all coalesce by that last night, so I could achieve the best possible result by the end of my stay. I had asked to understand the recurring snake imagery that seemed to haunt my unconscious, and I had had almost no snake visions my whole time down there, but that last night I went from a lifetime of being subjected to those visions to being given tools to work with "serpent power" productively. He was truly a "maestro," a conductor of psycho-spiritual energy whose personal style was to orchestrate, move and build energy, and then to deliver the goods in a grand finale.

My periodic forays into ayahuasca ceremonies since that episode a few years ago still on occasion feature some serpent (and some bird) imagery, but quite a lot less, and, in general, the experiences are far less visual than the psychedelic experiences of my youth. It may simply be that the visionary capacity of a human being diminishes with age, just like other faculties, but it may also be that, past a certain point, the experience becomes less about one's personal demons and specific neuroses and ambitions and spiritual seeking and more about an archetypal communion with the essence of life, with the heart's yearning for deep integrity and personal truth as one's life

enters its later stages. It seems to become, for me at least, a more pared down quest for pure light, or at least a making peace with one's inevitable return to the void and to the matrix of life we all come from. Of course, everyone's experience is different, so it's hard to generalize. I am getting to an age at which the physical ordeal is beginning to outweigh the psycho-spiritual benefits. I still feel rejuvenated in the weeks and months following my now increasingly infrequent immersions in that world, but I sense that the psychedelic part of my life is winding down. I certainly don't recommend these journeys to most people. The land of the serpents is definitely not for everyone.

Animal Encounters

Ungulates

Deer

Deer are now so numerous (apparently far more plentiful than in the 19th Century and even than in the pre-colonization period) in many parts of the U.S. that they are viewed as pests, the bane of gardeners and the cause of countless car accidents. Because I was raised in the city and never saw any in my environment as a child, once I became aware of them, they always fascinated me. I was amazed by the fact that such big wild animals could be so numerous so close to massive human populations. One could even at times see small herds of them grazing alongside the New York State Thruway. Most people in my region find them totally unremarkable, but to visitors from places with far less wildlife, their presence evokes wonder. When she was a child on one of her first visits here my French goddaughter marveled at seeing animals so rare in most of the European countryside right in the backyard of the upstate house we were all staying in. Despite their numbers and the countless times I have seen them, I always feel a certain excitement in their presence. They are high strung and furtive, but overall I find them to be very elegant creatures.

While reading spiritually themed books in my adolescence I

several times came across the mention that the Buddha had given his first public teachings at a "deer park" near Benares. I had always wondered what a "deer park" might be. I think I discovered the answer at a sort of hippie/new age hot springs resort in northern California that I dearly love and have been frequenting once or twice a year for some 35 years. The intentional community that runs the place absolutely forbids hunting on its extensive lands, so the deer have gradually understood that they are safe in this sanctuary, and over the years they have become so numerous and habituated to the unthreatening humans there that they graze nonchalantly all over the lawns and hillsides, often just feet away from picnickers or nude sunbathers. I do worry about some aspects of this interspecies cohabitation: that Lyme disease-transmitting ticks may be more plentiful, that mountain lions or other predators attracted by the plentiful game may at some point come too close to human habitations and put children at risk, and above all that the too numerous deer may denude the vegetation, especially along the stream banks, and contribute to flood damage and mud slides at some point in the future in a bad storm during the rainy season. But there is something Edenic about the presence of these deer (and more recently the bands of wild turkeys that now also freely roam this property). I can't explain it, but the fact that these animals don't feel threatened by me or the other humans in that place fills me with a certain pride and joy, a living proof that we can perhaps, at least at times, live in accordance with the higher angels of our nature. I now understand how fitting it is that Buddha first shared his wisdom in a "deer park."

Ungulates

The Big Elk

I was on a backpacking trip with a couple of friends in the High Uintas in Utah, the only significant mountain range in the U.S. with an east/west (rather than a north/south) orientation. We were in a fairly remote part of this already not very visited region in early to mid June, the beginning of the 6 to 8 week window during which the snow on the high passes melts enough to let summer hikers through. We were very possibly the first people up that way in many months, probably since the previous fall's hunting season.

One morning, I got up before my companions and decided to take a little stroll from the campsite we had established the night before, just to get my muscles moving before breakfast and to scope out the terrain in the narrow high valley we were in. It was a beautiful morning, not a cloud in the sky, and wonderfully quiet. I was strolling along a little absent-mindedly but feeling great when I approached a thicket of trees and turned a corner, and suddenly I was standing less than 10 feet away from the biggest ruminant I had ever seen. I had seen moose up in Maine and Canada and elk in Rocky Mountain National Park and Yellowstone grazing nonchalantly, even near the roads, but this guy had immense antlers and seemed to me to be the size of a pickup truck, and I was almost close enough to feel his breath. He must have been chewing on some bark or

grass and I obviously completely surprised him. His head sprung up and he stared at me but didn't move the rest of his body. I also didn't move. I was totally caught off-guard and my heart was pounding, but I immediately realized that if he lowered his head and charged, I was toast, so when he froze, I froze. It might have lasted seconds, but it felt like a really long time. Suddenly he bolted and was gone.

I heard the sound of branches breaking for a few moments as he ran off, but then not a sound. And suddenly, after a near heart attack, my attitude changed to curiosity. This valley had some small stands of trees, a few small boulders strewn about and a few thickets of bushes and high grasses hither and yon, but by and large it was open meadow. I looked around and couldn't see any movement of any kind. I took out my binoculars, climbed a high rock and scoured the landscape: nothing. I couldn't see any animals or detect any motion, and no sound betrayed the presence of a large mammal. I just couldn't fathom how you could hide an animal the size of a tractor in that fairly sparsely vegetated terrain, especially one who had to be close by, since it was such a narrow valley. Well, I guess you don't get to be such a big elk if you're not good at hiding from human hunters. I felt bad that I had spooked him, but I rationalized it by speculating that maybe I had helped prolong his life. Perhaps that encounter helped boost his alertness. Above all, I'm deeply grateful that he chose flight and not fight, or my own trajectory would have ended 35 years ago in the High Uintas.

Hayao Miyazaki's extraordinary animated eco-parable, *Princess*

Mononoke, which came out many years after this encounter, features a red elk very prominently, and also another elk/ibex/unicorn-like creature which is the embodiment of the spirit of the forest. It is one of my favorite films. I would have liked it anyway, but I suspect my run-in with the elk primed me to be enamored of it.

Animal Encounters

The Mysterious Cow

I first became aware of cows during my aforementioned year living in Switzerland as a child. They are ubiquitous in the mountains there, and most of them wear big bells that clang away as they move their heads and amble along. That sound and the pervasive smell of cow shit are iconic features of the Alpine and Jura regions. More recently, when I was last in Switzerland, I had taken the train from Milan to Basel, and I had noticed how many cows there still were throughout the country, and I asked a good friend there what proportion of the Swiss economy was agricultural and related to cattle, and he laughed and said: "It's just expensive landscaping." The country, he said, earns its currency by shady banking, watch making, pharmaceuticals and chemicals, but its identity is wrapped up in a nostalgic attachment to its rural past, and therefore to the ubiquitous presence of cows and meadows, so it subsidizes the sector very generously.

In any case, as an urban dweller most of my life, I've never had much direct, personal contact with cows. I've watched cows being milked, but I've never done it myself. I've petted a few, but it was hard to tell if they got any pleasure out of it. Like almost everyone else, I've seen countless cows as I was driving by range and farmland or riding in trains through rural areas, but that was about it. Once when I was car camping with a

Ungulates

friend near the San Francisco Peaks in Arizona, a herd of cows surrounded us as we were folding up our tent, and they wouldn't let us move. We started to try to begin walking, but they got agitated and blocked our way. For a good half an hour we had to stay fairly still and wait till they strolled off before we could get to our car a mere 30 yards away. It was a minor annoyance but still a humbling, even a humiliating experience.

But I did have one far more dramatic incident involving a cow. It was in the very late 1970s or very early 80s (sorry about the fuzzy dates, but I've never kept a journal, so I'm forced to depend on distant, approximate memories), during a year in which I had had to leave home fairly quickly because some business dealings I had gotten involved in had turned sour, and some of the other parties involved were, to be blunt, ruthless gangsters. I was extremely desirous of avoiding them as well as various branches of the constabulary who had been sniffing about, so I felt I needed to make myself scarce. I got hold of a car, arranged to have my bills and other affairs handled in my absence, and hit the road. During that year, I stayed away from New York. I took long drives to check in on friends throughout the country, visited a number of sites and towns I had long wanted to see, and mostly camped out in national forests along the way. I spent a lot of time mulling over my future and how to change my life, and periodically called contacts back home to explore if and when it might be safe to return.

I had eventually made it out to California and had rekindled a relationship with an on again/off again long distance girlfriend. When I finally got word that I could return safely and

Animal Encounters

it became time for me to make my way back home, she decided to take some time off from her work and accompany me for part of my slow drive back east. That trip became a very strange Odyssey. Our relationship was fairly rocky to begin with, and the weather and other factors seemed to reflect our inner jaggedness. To cite only one of many surreal episodes, as we were driving through a dramatic lightning storm near Lone Pine, California, we looked for lodging and followed signs to an old motel up a long dirt road up into the foothills. It turned out to be a series of old, nearly crumbling cabins in high desert, with not a soul around except the owner, a very old woman, who had been a star of westerns with Tom Mix during the silent film era, some of which had been made right on this property. She had photos from the film shoots lining the walls of her office. We were tired of driving and took pity on her, so, even after she warned us to watch out for rattlesnakes, we decided to stay at her "motel" and spent a sleepless night in a crumbling cabin as tumbleweeds and mini dust storms blew around all night, doors kept slamming in the wind, and everything creaked loudly.

The next day, as we continued our ride east, we picked up a hitchhiker who told us he had been at a rock festival in 1969 and had taken too big a dose of acid and had wound up in a mental hospital, and had only just then been released, some 12 years later. He was asking us what we thought he should do with his life. At that stage in my own trajectory, I was the wrong person to ask, as I hadn't a clue as to what to do with mine. He was a sweet fellow and obviously very vulnerable and lost, and I felt really sad for him. My companion was far more cynical

about the "acid casualty" and found the situation comical. She was very smart and funny, but she had a very harsh side as well. After we dropped him off, we fought about our differing views on compassion. And so it went.

We made our way to Arizona and visited the Navajo and Hopi reservations, including the spectacular but remote Canyon de Chelly. As it was getting late and we were hoping to get to a town and find some lodging, I had been driving pretty fast. As we passed an old Native man walking by the side of the road, he turned and stared. My friend was later convinced he was some sort of shaman/brujo who had placed a curse on us (like most of us back then, she had read way too much Carlos Castaneda). After a while, she took over the driving. It had been a beautifully clear fall day, not a cloud in the sky, when suddenly it began snowing and got very cold. Very rapidly the snow became thick and visibility very, very poor. We considered pulling over but drove on, though more slowly. I heard her scream: "There's a cow in the road. I'm going to hit it." And, sure enough, we did. Wham. The front end of the Volvo was seriously impacted: the radiator had been smashed; the car wasn't drivable. The freak snowstorm was blowing hard. I looked around but couldn't see the cow through the swirling snow. It had to be dead or badly injured, but it was nowhere around, and it was just too cold and windy to explore more extensively. My friend flagged down some Navajo guys in a pick-up truck on the way to a high school basketball game and headed off to get help. The guys looked pretty tough, but she was fearless, and I figured it would be worse for me to go and to leave her alone in the car, and somebody had to keep watch

over our stuff. I huddled in the freezing car with steam rising off the engine and the burst radiator and waited quite a while.

Eventually she showed up with the Navajo tribal police. As they drove us down toward the town of Window Rock, the snow disappeared within a few miles. It was all clear again. It had been a highly localized storm, our own personal mini blizzard. We had to spend two days in Window Rock as a minor Kafkaesque bureaucratic nightmare ensued. It turned out the road we had been on was almost exactly on the Arizona/New Mexico border: which side we had been on and which side the cow had come from and wound up on would influence which jurisdiction we had been in, which forms we needed to fill out etc., and no one could quite figure it out. And no one could find the cow or determine whose it might have been.

We left all the legal affairs in limbo. I arranged for my friend to get to an airport to go back out to San Francisco, and we were both relieved when we parted. I then had to have my car towed a few hundred miles to Santa Fe where I had good friends. It was the first of a handful of long rides I've had with tow truck operators, and it was eye opening. The few of these guys I've met had seen so many mangled bodies and met so many people during the worst moments of their lives that they had developed a deeply philosophical take on life. Their sense of the landscape was also radically different than mine. Where I saw an interesting rock formation, the tow truck driver saw the site of a massive tractor-trailer crash that had killed three back in 1974. Where I saw a stand of cottonwoods in a bend in the road, he pointed out the small white crosses for five

teenagers who died on the way home from their senior prom some five years before, etc. In a way reminiscent of Aboriginal song-lines, the highways were for him embedded with the history of all the tragedies he had been called upon to clean up the aftermath of over the decades.

Ultimately, one of my oldest friends in Santa Fe introduced me to some low-riders and bikers from Española who fixed my car at a very reasonable rate. Like all great populist mechanics, they improvised, and, not finding the right Volvo parts, they installed a refrigerator grill with a Westinghouse symbol on the front of my car. After a series of further adventures, including, not sure if I was hallucinating from sleep deprivation, narrowly missing herds of antelopes in the middle of the night as they raced across a very lonely road in west Texas, enduring a smashed windshield on my way to a New Orleans Blues festival, etc., it took quite a while, but I ultimately made it back to NYC, with a very funky, beat-up car, whose engine nonetheless still ran well.

A day or two after my return, I decided that I needed to pamper my weary body. I was exhausted and stressed from my rocky return trip. I went to the then main "alternative" health center in the city, the East/West Center for Holistic Health. They had an isolation tank that I spent two hours in, floating in complete darkness. Then I received a massage and some shiatsu and probably another treatment or two that I've forgotten, one after the other—the holistic therapies kitchen sink. No one, they said, had ever done all those things in one visit. It was excessive, but I finally felt really relaxed. A few hours later I

was stuck in traffic on the BQE (Brooklyn-Queens "Expressway") when I felt a huge shock and heard smashing steel and glass. A school bus driver, who claimed his brakes had failed, had rear-ended me. He wasn't going very fast, but it was a big bus, and it did a lot of damage. I had whiplash and a mild concussion, and the car was pretty much toast. The impact with the cow had done some damage to the car and a little bit to my body as well, but it's almost always our fellow humans (especially when they're equipped with technological artifacts), not other animals, who do the most damage.

I interpreted all those accidents and surreal episodes that marked the end of my 20s as the universe beating me on the head until I understood that I needed to radically change my life. That road trip provided the final catalyst. I had dabbled before, but after that I began the serious work of letting go of quite a few of my more blatantly self-destructive patterns. And the incident with the cow was really pivotal. I hope the hardcore secular rationalists among you pardon my flirting with magical thinking, but part of me does wonder if it had been some sort of paranormally induced storm meant only for us, and the cow some sort of shape-shifting spirit that dematerialized once its work was done. But where my then companion had seen a curse sent by a vengeful sorcerer because we had been driving too fast through sacred land and thereby exhibited thoughtlessness and disrespect, I wonder if it wasn't perhaps also a compassionate spell, sent to finally, unequivocally separate two people who really didn't belong together, and to help shock at least one of them awake. It definitely made me a better environmentalist by radically limiting my lifetime carbon footprint: I've never owned another car.

Equines

I admire their strength and robust elegance, but I've never really been into horses. I was led around on a pony in a cowboy suit at a theme birthday party my parents organized for me when I was around six or seven, and the old photos seem to indicate I was having a good time, but not long after that when they sent me to get riding lessons one summer when we were visiting relatives in Belgium, the riding teacher was barking orders and wielding a whip, and he really traumatized me. The few other times I attempted to ride the beasts in adulthood, it really hurt my testicles. I'm sure one learns how to avoid that problem, but I just decided I didn't enjoy riding on animals. I don't really like things moving under me. I never mastered skis or ice or roller skates. I don't really love boats, other than canoes. I don't like flying, especially in small planes that bounce all over the place. It's one reason I enjoyed running and love hiking and practice t'ai chi: all those activities are about one's relationship to reliably solid terra firma. The few earthquakes I've been in really unsettled me, because that last reliable thing—the solid ground, that even when I've been the most stoned or ill or miserable, was there supporting my body, could no longer be trusted.

One of my nieces cares for horses as a fulltime profession down in South Carolina. During one of my rare visits, I volunteered to help her out by shoveling up just one day's worth of

Animal Encounters

horseshit from three or so horses out in the meadow they were fenced into. I figured it would go fast. It took hours of back-breaking work. I also tend to associate horses with snotty rich people. When I went to school near Central Park and hung out there a lot, I'd see prissy young ladies in their riding gear, funny pants that balloon out and silly leather helmets and crops, trotting around the bridal paths, and one would read about scandals involving rich socialites in the Hamptons cheating on their husbands with Argentine gigolo polo players. And the fact that my father would comment, every time the result of the Kentucky Derby or Preakness or Belmont or some other high-stakes horse race was announced on the news: "That horse just made more money in two minutes than I've made in my entire life" probably also led me to unconsciously associate horses with inordinate wealth.

Another negative connotation I have with horses is that in many of the mountain regions I have backpacked in over the years there are outfitters who take people into the wilderness on horseback via the same trails we humble pedestrians have to take, and when they show up on the trail, we're the ones who have to get out of the way. Furthermore, very often these horses tear up the trails and can make them very muddy, and the big parties that come in on horseback frequently establish big campsites in the choicest spots along streams and lakes, clear a lot of vegetation and cut a lot of wood and therefore do a fair amount of damage. In the worst instances they leave a lot of litter, and it's irritating for those of us who have to carry all our own gear and food to watch these folks gorge themselves on steaks and beer. To be fair, there are quite a few places in

which the outfitters are very responsible and the relationship between walkers and riders isn't too bad, and I have to admit that in recent years, as my hiking friends and I age, we have on a few occasions rented a mule from an outfitter to take our packs in on the first day of a trip so we can get acclimated to hiking at altitude, and we've been grateful that an outfitter could provide us with that service and very grateful to the mule as well of course. I've come around to realizing that responsible outfitters can bring in people who otherwise couldn't enjoy being in the wilderness, and I don't begrudge them that experience. In some places a growing number of older hikers or family groups with children use llamas to bring in their gear. Llamas don't chew up the trails as they weigh less and have padded hooves that don't tend to damage trails, but they are expensive to rent, and one can't ride them. They only carry gear. It's definitely a bit of a surreal sight when one runs into a train of llamas on the trail.

In my younger days I briefly dated a real farm girl from Ohio who participated in county fair sheep-shearing contests and was a seasoned rider of farm horses. She described to me an experience she had when she was given the opportunity to ride a thoroughbred, explaining that it was akin to riding a Formula One Ferrari instead of the usual pick-up truck. I could feel the thrill of it in her telling, so I can see the appeal of horses on some level. I get the whole erotically charged, young girl/horse thing. I have enjoyed reading accounts of the riding feats of Plains Indians in their heyday or of Mongol warriors. I certainly have nothing against them and wish them all the best, but I just don't feel any personal, visceral connection to hors-

es, which probably explains why I've had a couple of frightening experiences involving equines.

Walking through a pasture in the Jura in Switzerland near the French border after buying some honey from a local beekeeper, a friend was telling me a whole, long obscene joke, and just as he was getting to the punch-line, some horses charged us. At first it seemed funny, but it got scary and we had to run as fast as we possibly could to just leap over a fence to avoid getting trampled or bitten. I have no idea what got them so riled up. He told me the punch line once he regained his breath.

I had a scarier incident during a driving trip below the Mason-Dixon Line. I was passing through Ocracoke, one of the narrow barrier islands off the North Carolina coast, which is known, among other things, for its herds of wild ponies. I had missed the last ferry and had to spend the night in a motel on the island. I went for a jog on the beach just after sunset. After a couple of miles, I saw some scurrying dark shapes about a quarter mile up ahead, darting between the dunes and the water's edge. It was hard to see in the penumbra, and I suffer from myopia and astigmatism, which makes night vision especially bad. My first thought was that there might be drug smugglers loading a boat or something, so I slowed down just to avoid waltzing into trouble. I got somewhat closer and still couldn't make out what was going on. Then suddenly some shapes emerged from the dunes and came right at me, and a small herd of some half dozen ponies surrounded me. If I began to move, even slightly, the one I got the sense was the leader of the band made some threatening neighing sounds,

showed its teeth and got up on its hind legs, which encouraged the others to paw the ground and stir, menacingly. They were just a few feet away from me. They had in fact herded me. I stood totally still. This lasted quite a while. It felt far more threatening than the similar incident with the cows in Arizona, because in that episode I hadn't sensed any real conscious hostility on the part of the cows, just some sort of instinctual mob behavior that had temporarily engulfed us. These ponies seemed far more purposeful. This was a conscious tactical maneuver to neutralize a potential threat. I realized I had to be as unthreatening as possible. I tried to do a Taoist standing meditation exercise, slowing my breath down. Finally the leader trailed off back inland and his troupe followed. They were impressive. I had just come stumbling through their turf, and they had made me understand with a deft military maneuver that, on this beach, on this island, I was definitely not the top mammal.

Animal Encounters

Aquatic Mammals

The Seal

I have seen plenty of seals in my life: a handful at zoos, big groups of them hanging out on the boat piers in San Francisco and at Seal Rock near Ocean Beach in that same town, solitary ones swimming a few hundred feet away at various East Coast beaches, even the gigantic elephant seals that congregate at Año Nuevo State Park near Santa Cruz that you can walk right up to and touch when they're exhausted after mating. But I have only had one very close encounter with one in the water.

I was spending a weekend with a group of friends. We knew each other through our participation in radical political activism in the late 1960s/early 1970s, and now it was more than 20 years later, so this reunion was thematically reminiscent of the film *The Big Chill* (or actually far more similar to the lesser known but earlier, far more realistic, and much better John Sayles film, *The Return of the Secaucus Seven*). Some of us had stayed in touch regularly, but we rarely gathered all together in one place. I don't remember what precipitated it or how we all wound up down in Southern California at the same time, but we were all staying up in Topanga Canyon at a house

Animal Encounters

that belonged to one of our crew. One day we went hiking somewhere in the Coastal Range north of Malibu and then wound up afterwards at the beach at Leo Carrillo State Park. I remember the name of the beach because Leo Carrillo had played the sidekick of The Cisco Kid, Pancho, on a western I had sometimes watched on TV as a very young child in the 1950s. Apparently Carrillo was also an ardent conservationist, which, I assume, is why a beach was named after him.

A few of us had taken micro doses of LSD, just for old times' sake. I was among them. The dose was just enough to be energizing, only moderately mind altering but enough to liven one's mood considerably. My friends were involved in a conversation on the beach, but I really felt like swimming. It was one of those stunning Southern California sunny days, and the water, though a bit cold, felt great. Aided by the acid I felt stronger and bolder than usual, so I swam quite a bit farther out than I normally would. I was alone out in the ocean. No one else was swimming. Sea gulls were flying low off the water, and as I would rise with each wave swell, I would occasionally see them whizzing by just feet away when I reached the wave's crest, and that was fun, grooving among the birds out in the water.

After a while I looked back to the beach, probably some hundred yards away, and my friends seemed to be gesticulating and pointing. I assumed they were just waving to me and clowning around, when suddenly a giant furry brown and black fat torpedo emerged out of the water less than a body length away from me. I immediately thought "shark" and "I'm

dead," but then it dawned on me that sharks aren't brown and furry and don't tend to leap out of the water. Had it been a shark I most likely never would have seen it till one my legs was missing. The seal basically flew over me. It was just swimming north, occasionally leaping out of the water. My friends had seen one of its previous leaps; hence their attempt to warn me. I just happened to be a minor obstacle on the seal's path. It's a good thing it wasn't overly annoyed because seals can definitely bite, and this was a very big specimen.

My initial terror faded almost instantly, and I wanted to see the seal and follow its progress, so I looked all around, but it was nowhere to be seen. We humans are so pathetically limited out on the ocean without sonar or good underwater vision. We only see the surface of things. After it was clear that the seal was long gone, I felt a tinge of loneliness, as though a playmate had just left me alone in the sandbox.

Animal Encounters

Otters

For playfulness and sheer lovability, no animal comes close to otters, and I find the great declines in their numbers on the U.S.' west coast to be one of the most depressing of all the myriad collapses in biodiversity our era is so rife with. I've had the great pleasure of watching groups of them on a few occasions, and I've had two memorable experiences with this species.

In the late 1960s, at age 18, I hitchhiked to California, drawn to both the radical activism around Berkeley and, like so many others, to San Francisco, the countercultural Mecca of the time. I got a lot of what I was looking for: my first initiation to tear gas at the "People's Park" demonstrations in Berkeley, involvement in a dynamic though fraying radical movement, a lot of acid rock concerts in parks and venues such as the Family Dog and the Fillmore, a lot of drugs, living in the woods in Southern Oregon for a while, and some visits to such incredible California treasures as Yosemite and Big Sur.

In July 1969 I somehow wound up camping out on a remote, fairly inaccessible beach at Big Sur with a bunch of hippie kids I had just met, and we dropped some acid. One of the guys there went up on high rock with a small transistor radio to get better reception, and he eventually yelled down to us: "They

just landed on the Moon, man." I was so alienated from mainstream culture at that point that, outside of the Vietnam War and various liberation struggles around the globe, which I did pay a lot of attention to, I had lost track of most other news. I had vaguely heard that a big rock concert was going to take place that summer back on the East Coast somewhere (Woodstock), but it barely registered, and I definitely hadn't really been paying attention to NASA's exploits. The Moon Landing, predictably, blew the mind of the assembled psychonauts, who were whooping it up and mixing the acid with cheap wine. I have to admit I didn't really care that someone had gone to the Moon.

The next day I decided that this scene was too chaotic for me, so I hiked up the coast a few miles to an even remoter beach that could only be reached by racing around a protruding cliff at the peak of low tide, figuring I could have a few days of solitude there. I had enough food and there was plenty of driftwood to make campfires, and a small waterfall provided enough fresh water. It was truly an idyllic spot. There were some big masses of floating kelp that are quite common at Big Sur right offshore. I was out swimming near those kelp mats one afternoon, when I heard a lot of noise and splashing in the water. I turned and looked: it was a family of otters some 25 yards away or so. I tried to move gingerly and to be very unobtrusive, but they had noticed me and looked right at me, and then they just continued doing their thing, diving and frolicking and chasing each other with such gleeful abandon that I fell in love with otters forever. They hung out for a long time and some came up quite close to me. I was honored that they

didn't perceive me as a threat, and that they let me hang out while they partied.

My most endearing otter experience came some twenty years or so later. I was jogging alone on a long beach in Point Reyes National Seashore in Marin County, California. It was a chilly weekday in the fall. No one else was around. I had the beach all to myself, when an otter appeared maybe 15 yards offshore, splashing around. I almost got the impression he was waving to me. I checked him out for a little while and then resumed jogging. He proceeded to accompany me, swimming parallel to the shore very close to the beach, splashing gleefully as he went and definitely looking at me frequently. I kept expecting him to tire of it and to swim off to look for food or other otters, but he stayed with me all the way to the end of my run, a good five miles. There was absolutely no question that he was engaging with me. I'm sure wildlife biologists will sneer at my romantic anthropomorphism, but I can't think of any narrowly "Darwinian" reason for his behavior. There was no apparent evolutionary advantage to it. I am convinced that what I witnessed was pure love of play. In any event, it was the most joyous and exhilarating jog of my life.

Bears

Because I have backpacked quite a lot in areas in which bears are not uncommon (which, in North America, is most places a hiker is likely to go outside of deserts), I have had to be alert to their possible presence just about every time I have ventured into "wild lands." This means that I have whenever possible hung my food high from a tree branch at night, not taken food into my tent, and been alert to signs of bears. Given how often I have seen clear evidence of bear presence— still steaming bear shit, obvious prints and claw marks on trees, etc.— it is quite surprising how few bears I have actually seen. At the conclusion of one backpacking trip in the Sierras in California, when we got back to the parking lot there was a lot of hubbub because some car doors had been ripped off by bears looking for food. Fortunately our car was unscathed. On another occasion, at the end of a day-hike in the Cascades in Washington State, there were clear bear paw prints that definitely hadn't been there before on the dusty windows of our rented van. Again, luckily, my companions and I hadn't left anything edible in the vehicle, and the bear apparently just got up on its hind legs, looked in, and wandered off.

Outside of hiking, I have seen a few bears in other contexts, raiding a neighbor's bird feeder when I rented a place in

Animal Encounters

upstate New York, one walking across a road in Montana and one in Vermont, one small cinnamon-colored one ambling down a hill in Lake County, California, and a few raiding a bakery's dumpster off route 28A in Ulster County, NY. I had heard stories from friends about their packs being ripped open by bears up on the Pacific Crest Trail and local stories in Woodstock, NY of bears leaping into swimming pools or actually breaking into homes and opening the refrigerator, especially in drought years, and of course I have paid attention to the occasional bear horror stories reported by the media, but until some ten years ago I had had only had one close encounter with a bear, which I heard very clearly right outside my tent but never saw, while I was camped out during a meditation retreat.

During the early 1980s I was attending a weeklong Taoist meditation retreat with a few dozen other people in the Catskills region of upstate New York near the town of Kerhonkson. I didn't want to sleep in the fairly crowded dormitory-like conditions in the one building on the site, so I brought a small tent and pitched it quite a ways away from other people, a bit out in the woods. I can be charming and sociable, but I have some loner and misanthropic tendencies as well, and there's something about group activities that triggers a certain rebellious streak in me, so that, while I try to participate fully in the common work, I also feel the need to express my separation and individuality. In this instance it had already gotten me in trouble, because I had gone running through the woods (as far from my fellow meditators as possible) during a late afternoon period of "free time" in only shorts on what had been a warm day and managed to get totally lost. When I finally reached a

road, I realized I had no idea of the address of the house where the retreat was being held, as I had been driven there and hadn't needed that information. It took me quite a while to find someone in this sparsely populated rural area who recognized the name of the person whose property the retreat was being held at, who kindly gave me a ride back, and by then it was dark and cold, and I was late for dinner and the butt of much ribbing.

I had brought a few food items to the retreat: some coffee that I could make with a small camping stove, and some nuts and dried fruit and other healthy snacks, just in case I needed an energy lift at some point. Even though, as an experienced hiker, I never leave food in my tent in bear country, I did in this case because I wasn't approaching this stay the way I would a wilderness trip. I was so focused on the retreat and the practices we were learning that I lost sight of the fact that though I wasn't far from a house and from a lot of other people I was still sleeping in the woods.

The complex meditative disciplines we were working with included a range of breathing techniques, ways to speed up or slow one's heartbeat as well as to gain more conscious control of the nervous, lymphatic and other bodily systems, very elaborate visualizations, the use of special sounds to tone one's internal organs, classic Taoist "energy circulation" methods which involve directing highly focused attention on a number of the "meridians" used in acupuncture, and a whole slew of other related practices, including some vigorous internal martial arts training exercises. It was quite intense work for 8 to 10 hours a day. One of the meditative techniques had a shaman-

ic flavor in that it involved visualizing archetypal animals and seeking to draw the desirable attributes of those animals into our own consciousness to bolster our mental strength and our martial arts skills. Now I worked with the images of several animals, but I wound up focusing especially on bears. I guess that since bears were the most impressive, top-of-the-food chain, big animals in the ecosystem I was in, focusing on their attributes made sense. In any case it's what entered my mind first when I was told to visualize an "animal spirit."

Toward the middle of the week, late at night as I was sleeping in my tent, I suddenly woke up. It felt to me as though my body had been intensely practicing the meditative techniques we had been working with. I felt waves of "chi" racing through all my meridians and hyper-activating my "chakras." I felt as though the intensity of the chi flow had woken me up, but then I heard really loud cracking branches and footsteps and very heavy breathing, and definitely not human breathing, very close to my tent. And then it got right up to my tent. At first I thought I was in the throes of some mystical experience. I had somehow conjured the bear spirit I had been visualizing in deep meditation, but then I realized very quickly that no, this was a real, noisy bear attracted by the smell of the food I had so stupidly kept in my tent. I tried not to move a muscle, but then I decided I needed to do something, so I felt for the small flashlight I kept near my head and turned it on, pointing in the general direction of where I sensed the bear was, hoping it might confuse or disorient it enough to dissuade it from converting my tent into a body bag and me into a corpse. I heard the bear amble away. Bear attacks are exceedingly uncommon

on the East Coast, though one of the few deadly incidents to occur in the Eastern U.S. in the last few decades (in 2002) involved the death of a toddler and took place not far from Kerhonkson.

Another bear-related episode occurred during a trip to the Mountain West that I took with a new girlfriend in the summer of 1984. She was a super-fit aerobics teacher, so I figured she might enjoy backpacking, which she had never done, but far more important than being fit is the capacity to endure discomfort (bugs, cold and wet conditions, rapid weather changes, steep ascents and descents, scrapes, burns, having to shit in the woods, etc.). One either has to have such a passionate yearning for untrammeled wilderness that the love of nature trumps the discomfort, or one has to take a sort of perverse, masochistic pride in one's capacity for intense effort and intentional suffering. It turned out that she wasn't in either of those two camps. We had already done one foray up into the Wind River Range in Wyoming, and it had been very rough emotionally. We were contemplating breaking up after that, even though we had fairly recently been passionately drawn to each other, but, hey we were still out West, and I convinced her to give it another shot. We went up to Montana, to the town of Big Sky, and got ready to go into the backcountry from there. She made me promise that we would not go anywhere grizzlies might be present, so we went to the ranger station and inquired. The ranger we spoke to assured us that they had a really good sense of where there were grizzlies, and she showed us on the map an area she thought we would enjoy going to that, she was certain, harbored none of those top predators.

Animal Encounters

We hiked in, and several hours later, I went down to a creek to refill our canteens. I saw several huge, fresh bear tracks in the mud. There was no way those were black bear paw marks. I kept this data to myself to avoid inducing panic and rage in my companion, but I took some extra precautions. At night I hung our food farther away than usual, and I kept our campfires quite a ways away from our tent, plus I made sure we didn't keep anything scented in the tent (sunscreen, chap-sticks, etc.), and so on. The four-day hike turned out to be fairly uneventful. When we got back to the town of Big Sky, though, the town was abuzz. While we had been in the woods, a young Olympic athlete, Keri Swenson, who had been jogging near Big Sky, right next to the trailhead we had begun our trip at, had been kidnapped at gunpoint by two "mountain men," a father and son, and dragged into the mountains. A rescue party found them soon after, but a rescuer was shot and killed and Swenson herself was wounded, while the abductors managed to flee into the wilderness. It took five months to find them and bring them to justice. The kidnapping and shootout happened very close to where we had been hiking. I'm surprised we never heard the gunshots, and we're lucky we didn't cross paths with the fleeing kidnappers, as I'm sure my girlfriend would have been every bit as appealing to them as Keri Swenson. One irony is that Swenson had been jogging in that area because someone had seen a grizzly there, and she had never seen one, and was hoping to catch a glimpse during her run. The lesson I took home from this episode was that, once again, bear horror stories aside, 99% of the time it's the humans you have to watch out for (and also that one should take forest rangers' assurances about their knowledge of animal behavior with many grains of salt…).

Bears

The one really scary, up-close-and-personal bear incident I've had in my life happened in British Columbia a decade or so ago. I was hiking with some very old, close friends in the Stein Valley, an area that had been the site of a long, major environmental battle over logging, that Canadian environmentalists and the local indigenous people (the Nlaka'pamux) whose ancestral land it is, had largely won. It's a fascinating place in that there are ancient petroglyphs there, and it's still used by the local native inhabitants for vision quests and sacred pilgrimages. One has to get a permit from the tribe to hike in, and certain parts of the area are off-limits. It definitely has the feel of a sacred landscape, and one sees signs of active worship, such as recent offerings, at specific spots, usually those with major petroglyphs. One site we came across with stunning, elaborate petroglyphs, had been very recently used for a pilgrimage. Someone had left cigarettes and condoms there in an obviously ritualized context. I know tobacco is frequently used as an offering in Native American religious practices, but I intuitively got the sense that the person who had left these objects was promising the spiritual powers to quit smoking and to discipline his sex life, though obviously that was pure speculation on my part. More relevantly to the theme of this text, the Stein Valley is also known as an area with a lot of wildlife, including black bears and grizzlies.

One of my oldest and closest friends, Adam Raskin, with whom I've gone on more backpacking trips than anyone, was really eager to visit the Stein because he had gone to college in Canada and had been politically active while there and had followed the battle over the area closely. One of his former col-

lege roommates lived in Vancouver, and this very interesting fellow and his wife, who were significant figures in local politics there (and also owned a cool jazz club), very graciously hosted us as we prepared for our expedition. Adam's wife Adelina, the person in the world I know with the most positive outlook and a really enthusiastic and experienced hiker as well (who is, however, bear phobic) and another very old friend, Chris Shea, completed our party.

The entire hike was along the Stein River, heading slowly up into the mountains. On our third day in, we were hiking in the late afternoon along a narrow trail surrounded by swampy and densely wooded impassable terrain on both sides. At one point we heard big branches breaking and I caught a fleeting glimpse of the hindquarters of a grizzly probably 50 or 60 yards away, but, fortunately, fleeing away from us. We hiked on. We were trying to get to the next viable campsite before darkness set in. I had brought a whistle to blow to warn bears off, and I kept it around my neck, close at hand. An hour or so later as we hiked up a small incline and turned a corner, I suddenly saw a small bear cub ten feet or so ahead on the ground and then another who scurried a few yards up a tree trunk. Immediately I knew we were in trouble. Mercifully, these were black bears, not grizzlies, but the momma bear could not be far, and suddenly there she was, no more than 20 yards away. She charged. One is always told not to run away from a bear. We ran like crazy. It happened very fast. It was purely instinctual. I never had time to blow my whistle.

After a mad dash of a hundred yards or so, we realized she wasn't following us. It had been what is called a "false charge."

Bears

I guess the way you know the difference between a "false charge" and a real charge is that if there's someone around telling you the story who isn't badly maimed, then it was a "false charge."

Anyway, we regrouped, panting, hearts pumping. What should we do? We needed to go further up that trail in order to make camp before dark. We decided to stay where we were and to make a lot of noise for a few minutes. Adam (among other things, a solid percussionist) began singing Afro-Cuban chants and pounding out a *clave* rhythm on a tree trunk. We all banged on trees and hollered, and I blew my whistle at length. We gathered up our courage and tried again, hoping the noise would have convinced the momma bear to take her cubs to a safer and quieter place, but she was still there in the same place, right on the trail. She charged again. Same result. This time we must have run 200 yards. Thankfully it had been another "false charge," but we weren't going to risk it again. We gave up and backtracked a long way till we could find a suitable campsite out of the swamps. We slept very nervously.

The next day as we were hiking, around midday, we found a very appealing spot by the river. It had a nice sandy beach and good views upstream. We decided to stop to have lunch. We hadn't run into any people since we had started our hike four days before, but we saw two women maybe a quarter mile away on what seemed like an island out in the river. They waved and we waved back. We were about to take our backpacks off, when suddenly we heard loud splashing in the river to our right, and saw an animal swimming toward us.

Animal Encounters

Someone yelled: "bear." Adelina ran off with her pack still on faster than I've ever seen anyone move. Adam and Chris began to bolt as well. I had already plopped myself down and was leaning against a tree with my very heavy pack still on. Instead of trying to get up, I began to frantically blow on my whistle. The animal stopped swimming, and I thought: "Wow. This "bear whistle" actually works." It swam back in the opposite direction. I began to realize that it was really too small to be a bear. Maybe it was a big dog or a coyote or something. We regrouped again and calmed down and began preparing lunch. About ten minutes later the two women came ambling down the trail with their wet dog, a small poodle. We had been panicking about a poodle. The two women were big and strong. They looked like rugby players. They were very friendly and told us they had camped nearby but had been out to that island in the middle of the river because they had seen grizzly tracks heading that way and really wanted to see one. Apparently everyone but my friends and I want to see bears. We felt like complete wimps. I am convinced that these Canadian amazons have been regaling their friends for years with the hilarious anecdote about the histrionic, wimpy Americans who ran screaming from a poodle.

Rodents

Mice, Rats, Rabbits, etc.

My main experiences with rodents and other rodent-like species have, totally predictably for a city dweller, been with mice, rats, squirrels, a handful of the now more common raccoons, who have made an urban comeback in some neighborhoods, the few pet hamsters some of my childhood friends had, and an occasional run-in with a skunk in the country. Growing up I also saw occasional rabbits along the highways in the suburbs that in the 1950s where I lived in Queens had just been converted from farmland and woods and paved over. I still, on rare occasions, occasionally see a rabbit in Prospect Park. I never had any phobia about rodents. I still find mice cute (even though I know they can, in rare instances, transmit the potentially lethal hantavirus) and it was very painful for me to have to set traps when they were too numerous in apartments I lived in, or when I've lived with cats who tortured them. In recent years a humane rodent control business in my neighborhood in Brooklyn run by a vegan goth/punk girl promises it removes and relocates mice outside the city. I wish she had been around years ago. And I know they can be disease vectors (the plague!) and that they terrorize children in poor neighborhoods, but I feel no hatred for rats when I see

them crawling along the subway tracks or scurrying around near construction sites. I have many fears, but I don't share that one with *1984's* Winston Smith. The movies *Willard* and *Ben* did not freak me out. None of my dealings with rats or mice have been all that dramatic or traumatic, other than perhaps having to watch a camp counselor drown four baby mice when I was a young camper.

Rodents

Squirrels

Squirrels are the liveliest animals we city folk encounter most frequently. I am grateful to them for providing at least a small sense of wildness, a tenuous link to a less tame world, even in our overbuilt human environment, though, ironically, they were actually intentionally introduced into urban parks starting in the 1840s, so their presence isn't exactly completely "natural." Of course not much on our planet is anymore, not in this age some have dubbed the Anthropocene Era.

When I was eight or nine I was taken squirrel hunting by the caretaker of a rich woman's estate on Long Island. My parents figured I should have that experience. It was the only time in my life I've been hunting. I fired my gun once and missed (and was so happy about that afterwards), but my guide shot two squirrels, and seeing their splattered corpses and their still lively if frozen facial expressions and expressive eyes filled me with horror. The unnecessary extinction of life's vital force in such small and innocent creatures who were so bursting with energy a moment before and had just been minding their own business seemed deeply, cosmically wrong, and it was especially incomprehensible because the old Italian fellow who took me on this outing was a sweet man who had always been kind to me. I had been happy to go off with him and the household's lovable dog in the early morning's bracing air with a sense of

purpose and adventure, so I was filled with cognitive dissonance. How could a nice person commit such a cosmic transgression? More than fifty years later I have, predictably, become deeply accustomed to that feeling of cognitive dissonance about so many realms of human behavior. As for nearly all of us, perhaps inevitably and maybe even necessarily, growing up and settling into adulthood has for me been accompanied by a habituation to all sorts of horrors, but the memory of that first heartbreaking, gut-wrenching shock of incomprehension, and the nausea of watching and participating in a killing, has stayed forever vividly etched in my mind's eye and seared in my soul.

It took me another two decades to become largely vegetarian, or at least someone who refuses to eat mammals except, during my travels, in the rarest of specific socio-cultural situations in which I have felt compelled to go along with local customs. I am not naïve. While nature features far more symbiosis and, in Prince Kropotkin's memorable phrasing, "mutual aid," than had until recently been acknowledged by most scientists, one still can't deny that the whole "nature red in tooth and claw" business is a big part of the equation, but killing for its own sake, for sport, is still incomprehensible to me, and Long Island isn't Tennessee; these folks definitely didn't eat squirrel brains.

I had a similarly painful experience on my one fishing attempt in childhood. I was thrilled when I finally hooked a fish and then disgusted with myself when I saw the fish flop around desperately and then eventually life leave its body. I guess I'm an effete wimp, but killing (other than of mosquitoes and other

Rodents

relentlessly biting insects) fills me with shame and revulsion. That said, I still occasionally eat fish, so I'm obviously somewhat of a hypocrite, or at least someone not fully capable of living up to his highest ideals. And there are definitely some human beings whose demises would not trouble me much, so I'm far from consistent in my worldview regarding life's sacredness.

Back to squirrels: In later years I "befriended" two different squirrels who regularly scampered along my window ledges in two different buildings I lived in. They sometimes stopped and stared at me working at a desk. In each case I began to on occasion leave them nuts on the ledge, and they became habituated to my presence and therefore a tiny bit less skittish, so I got to observe them quite close up for extended periods. I've also observed the ubiquitous squirrels in the city's parks and came to admire their extraordinary athleticism, especially their leaping abilities.

I had only ever seen grayish/brownish/slightly reddish squirrels in the city's parks, but about ten years ago I began seeing more black ones, which for some reason reminded me of how the appearance of dark Peppered Moths during the Industrial Revolution seemed to confirm Darwinian evolutionary theory, though there is surely absolutely no comparable evolutionary advantage to being a black squirrel in Brooklyn, as our trees are not darkened by soot as so much of England was in the 19th Century. But that might not be true of the one albino squirrel that created quite a stir when people first began noticing it in Prospect Park a few years back. It blew my mind when

Animal Encounters

I first saw it. I had never seen a white squirrel. It became the object of much discussion in the neighborhood when a red-tailed hawk tried to snag it and a young Park Slope mother left her stroller and chased the bird of prey away with an umbrella to save the rare snowy-hued rodent. Lively discussions on local blogs explored whether the squirrel's rare genetic mutation, which, in normal circumstances would have made it far too visible to predators to last long in the wild, actually conferred an adaptive advantage in an urban context because its whiteness and cuteness would elicit protective impulses from many of the very numerous, dominant big bipedal mammals in that environment. A fascinating discussion, but I haven't seen that squirrel or any other white ones in a few years, so the hawks probably won out in the end.

Rodents

Porcupines

I've seen just a few porcupines in my life, in the woods in upstate New York, and, for obvious reasons I gave them a wide berth. I've also seen a half dozen or more dead ones that had been run over by cars, and I knew at one time a family of Chinese artists who lived in Woodstock who on a couple of occasions removed the quills from road-killed porcupines they found to use in calligraphy and artwork. The parents, both from rural China, had apparently been taught how to do this in their homeland. But on two occasions, one humiliating and one heartbreaking, I had more charged encounters with porcupines.

The first was during a canoe and camping trip on Long Lake in the Adirondacks region of New York. There were four of us on the expedition, and that day we were a bit disorganized and had gotten a late start. Night was falling and it had taken us a while to find a suitable place to come ashore and put up our tents in that very densely forested area, so we were fumbling with our gear with almost no light, as we hadn't yet started a fire. Suddenly an animal was right among us, making very aggressive sounds. Of course our first thought was that it was a bear and we panicked and jumped back and reached for our flashlights, and it turned out, to our relief (at least initially), to be a porcupine. We figured multiple flashlights in its face and

four much bigger mammals yelling at it would drive it away. No such luck. At first it just stared us down and growled and hissed. When we made shooing sounds and movements, it charged toward whomever had made a threatening gesture, and we would leap away trying to get up higher on any rocks or logs we could find. This lasted a good ten minutes. It eventually left, ambling away slowly, taking its own sweet time, and, after a while, we chuckled about it, but it's a bit hard to savor the feeling of proudly returning to the wild woods like one's primal, archaic ancestors, when you've been intimidated and basically chased up a tree by a rodent.

The other incident dramatically changed my feelings about porcupines. During a roughly twenty-year period during which I spent parts of every summer in the Catskills, I spent a lot of time in probably my favorite place on Earth, a steep, heavily forested canyon (as they're called in that region, a "clove"— probably a derivation of an old Dutch term for a cleft in the mountains), carved out over the millennia by a marvelously gushing stream with a great variety of waterfalls and swimming holes. I still go there a few times a year on a pilgrimage of sorts. The first few years after I discovered the place, I almost never ran into any other humans up there. One had to trespass a bit and discreetly cross some private property to get into the state land, and other than a few local kids who occasionally went swimming in one of the first few deep and wide pools or the very rare fly fisherman, it was virtually unvisited. I had heard that some of the local old-timers feared the place because every once in a while someone died, slipping off one of the steep rocky slopes, and because there were old stories

about copperheads living up there. I went to that canyon a lot and explored, swam, and meditated under waterfalls, etc., and fell in love with the place, more than I have with any other spot on Earth.

Unfortunately some sociopathic locals used the canyon as a dump of sorts. They would, at night, drive their pick-up trucks filled with garbage up the very steep road that wound up one side of the "clove" and dump their trash over the edge of the cliffs so they wouldn't have to pay dump fees. People even sent cars over the edge to claim insurance money saying their vehicle was stolen or just to get rid of old cars. Some of the trash would, over time, despite the dense tree cover, drift down to the bottom of the clove, so, in this very wild and stunningly beautiful, almost Edenic wilderness, one of the most rugged parts of the East Coast, one would occasionally run across tires or even the occasional old refrigerator or washing machine, not to mention various bits of household garbage. And, over the years, sadly for me, the area got "discovered" and it became much more popular and some campsites got pretty badly trashed. I had developed a proprietary or at least a caretaker's mindset about the place, so I, along with a few other people, organized some efforts to clean out the worst trash, to appeal to visitors to be conscious, and to pressure the state's Department of Environmental Conservation to monitor it a little bit. Today the situation has improved somewhat, and it's still a stunning place where one can find real solitude at certain times of the year, but, like so much of the natural world, it's at risk.

But I have digressed: back to porcupines. In those early years of going into the clove, I had seen porcupines back up in the canyon a couple of times. I had also begun jogging up (and then back down) the aforementioned steep road at sunset every other day or so. These were the years of my prime fitness. That road is probably among the steepest in the Northeast, though only for some 2 miles, and I ran it slowly. Still, I can't imagine doing that now. One reason I had begun running up the road, besides the challenge and the spectacular views it afforded, was that at that point I was obsessed with protecting this canyon, and I was hoping that I might catch someone dumping garbage and get their license plate number. I knew the two or three preferred spots to dump. I never did catch anyone, but one evening, as I was approaching the biggest bend in the road about halfway up the incline, the one that afforded the most sweeping view of the surrounding mountains and the Hudson River Valley below, and that also happened to be a prime trash-dumping site, I saw the mangled body of a porcupine in the middle of the road; it had obviously been hit by a car. Then I saw another porcupine by the side of the road, very agitated, pacing back and forth and in circles, making noises that sounded to me to be the equivalent of human wailing. I assumed it was the dead porcupine's mate, and I was deeply saddened and moved. The mourning porcupine was still there when I came back down the road a half hour or so later. Two evenings later I ran up the road again, and to my astonishment the porcupine was still nearby, this time part of the way up a tree near the side of the road, continuing its display of grief. It had stayed near the body of its mate for 48 hours at least. The tenacity and intensity of its emotions were gut wrenching. No

Rodents

one who witnessed what I did could ever believe, as Descartes did, that animals are mere machines. The older I get the less I understand, but one thing I know unequivocally is that porcupines mourn their dead.

Animal Encounters

Birds

I was never heavily interested in birds. Because they're the most common form of non-human life that even urban dwellers see every day, and because their numbers are so great, many of us take them for granted. We also tend to vilify some of the most common urban species, such as pigeons, crows, starlings, etc., viewing them, sometimes for good reasons, as nuisances. When I take the time to really think about birds, their ability to fly above the rest of us, to soar on thermals and to perch on terrifyingly steep buildings or cliffs or trees blows my mind, but I've never been able to stay focused on them for too long.

Even thinking about a creature that can fly so high and doesn't experience any vertigo makes me dizzy, and after a short while I have to return my attention to ground level where my mammalian life takes place. I have friends into bird watching and one who is an ace hang-glider pilot and gets to observe them close up in the air, but I've never been able to match these friends' level of enthusiasm, though a bunch of bird-related nature shows on TV have held my attention, and I've certainly had quite a few encounters with birds, as I suspect most of us have. They are numerous and ubiquitous enough that we inevitably have to interact with them in some fashion.

Animal Encounters

And don't get me wrong: I'm not totally insensitive to their charms: I have been excited to see a number of hawks and ospreys and even a few eagles, both perched and in flight in various locales. I've been thrilled the couple of times I saw a solitary blue heron standing in a wild stream. I've watched ravens soaring elegantly above the slopes of Mount Tamalpais north of San Francisco and in many other places. My father took me when I was a young child to the town of Grasse in southern France, renowned for its perfume distilleries, to see its also famous flocks of swallows swirl in amazing formations at dusk. I've jogged on many beaches and been amused watching the plovers and other shorebirds sprint comically en masse to avoid the waves. I went to check out the famous flock of parrots that has established itself on Telegraph Hill in San Francisco about whom a movie has been made, as well as another flock descended from escaped imported parrots, this one closer to home, near Greenwood Cemetery in Brooklyn.

I've had to escape from a huge "murder" of crows when a foolish dog I was walking in Golden Gate Park pissed them off. In the Gila Wilderness in Southern New Mexico where I was helping some friends work on an experimental biodiversity farm project, I took a stroll one evening. I walked under a big cottonwood tree alongside the Gila River and had an eerie feeling and looked up, and there were hundreds of crows massed all over its branches, like a bumper crop of very big, feathered, jet-black fruit, staring at me, totally quiet. I mentally apologized for invading their space and backed out of there with slow, smooth movements. I've been pecked and dive-bombed by various species of birds in both city parks and

Birds

friends' gardens when I must have come too close to their nests. Once, while jogging in Prospect Park in the penumbra just past sunset, I was coming through a thicket of trees when I saw a large animal in front of me. I wasn't wearing glasses, and I have pretty lousy night vision, so I initially thought it was a big, skinny dog. It was a big red-tailed hawk, and I had really surprised it. It panicked and flew up right in my direction. I ducked and it missed me by perhaps a foot. There are quite a lot of hawks and falcons in the city these days, and even some wild turkeys and owls at times in Central Park. I even heard a woodpecker one season in Prospect Park, but I think some Central American practitioners of an indigenous religious tradition killed it for its feathers. I saw them stalking it and climbing trees to find its nest. I wanted to talk them out of it and plead the bird's case, but there were five of them, and they had machetes, and the cultural chasm felt too deep to bridge in that context. In general though, global biodiversity is definitely plummeting, but there are way more bird species in the city's parks than when I was growing up.

On one occasion, probably in the late 1970s, I had just started learning t'ai chi and I was trying to practice in Fort Greene Park in Brooklyn. It was taking me a while to start feeling relaxed and centered. I thought I was finally getting there, when I heard some frantic but brief squawks above my head. I looked up and saw that a hawk had just snagged a pigeon in mid flight, and a few bloody feathers slowly drifted down to the ground right next to me. I took this to be a lesson about the importance of keeping reality firmly in mind, even while engaging in meditative practices, especially in that part of

Animal Encounters

Brooklyn, which, in those days, was still very far off from the ultra hip, upper middle class playground it has since, at least in part, become.

I've also run into some interesting examples of bird-human relationships. Back in the 1970s I had some dealings with a clan of six Polish brothers who were pot dealers in the Greenpoint neighborhood of Brooklyn and were also racing pigeon aficionados. They insisted on conducting business discussions on the roof of their tenement building as they tended to their flocks, and I got to observe some very well treated pigeon athletes in action. A woman I worked with for a while in an holistic adult education center had two small canaries she would let fly throughout the building and that would often perch on her shoulder even as she typed away on her computer. While in Italy visiting the Italian branch of my family, I attended a dinner party at the home of an incredibly refined, wealthy but very eccentric Milanese socialite, world traveler and art collector who had two large parrots who had the run of the apartment and came up on the table pecking away at peppers and talking among the guests. I remember one of them repeatedly saying: "Ciao amore" to all and sundry.

I did have one truly transcendental experience involving a bird. I had always thought hummingbirds were extraordinary creatures—the blinding speed of their wing movements, their amazing ability to hover, their unbelievable stamina in long distance flight, their exquisitely shaped beaks, ideally suited for the specific flower or plant each subspecies specializes in, their stunning plumage and coloring, etc., etc. I was on a group

Birds

retreat quite a few years ago in the mountains of northern New Mexico, and one of the other participants was a remarkable naturalist, environmental activist, ornithologist, and all-around polymath genius, Peter Warshall, who, very sadly, just died last year. Peter, whose fully engaged life included studying at the Sorbonne with Claude Lévi-Strauss, being the informal "mayor" of the once notorious hippie enclave of Bolinas, California and the editor of the Whole Earth Review for many years, flying to Rome to lobby the Vatican along with Arizona indigenous leaders to save the endangered Mount Graham Squirrel (a long story), working to protect jaguars in the desert southwest of the U.S. and Mexico, and far too many other noble projects worldwide to list here, also had, among so many domains of expertise, probably as much knowledge about hummingbirds as anyone on the planet.

We were on a walk at that isolated, high mountain retreat one afternoon and spotted one, and he knew immediately exactly which of some three hundred subspecies it belonged to, what it was doing there, the plant species it pollinated, where it wintered, its migratory route, etc. He proceeded to regale me with a lot of mind-blowing data and lore regarding these tiny but mind-bending birds. Peter's passion for hummingbirds always stayed with me and made me even more excited when I would see one, but that was a very rare occurrence. I once saw one on my block in Brooklyn, which does have a number of gardens in front of some houses, but it still blew my mind and seems to have been an isolated incident, as I've never seen another one here on my street.

Animal Encounters

One summer I went on a backpacking trip in California's Sierras, in the Emigrant Basin Wilderness, an area north of Yosemite I dearly love. There is a lot of that smooth granite that Ansel Adams photographs have made the Sierras so famous for and there are many lakes up there, and it's not all that traveled. You can get to some very isolated lakes and sometimes have them all to yourself for days on end if you're good at bushwhacking (because it is easy and dangerous to get lost up there if you're not experienced at backcountry travel). One of my companions on this trip was a friend I had known for many years, but we had somehow stumbled into being lovers during this particular period. It seemed pretty obvious this was a temporary arrangement, and there was some tension involved, but it was mostly fun while it lasted. After a few days of hard hiking we made it to one of my favorite spots—a beautiful lake ringed by smooth granite cliffs, one that has one of the only white sand beaches in the Sierras. We set up camp.

The next day was stunningly clear, the sky a shade of impossibly bright blue. A soft, delicious cool breeze created gentle ripples on the lake's surface and made the leaves on the aspen trees that lined the shore quake more sensually than usual. The sand was warm. The two of us wound up at midday alone on the beach, and, though we had squabbled somewhat during the previous few days, given the beautiful setting and the gorgeous weather, we got deeply relaxed, and, predictably, began to have sex. In this instance I was on top and she below. As my partner was getting increasingly stimulated, and a climax seemed imminent, I heard a fluttering sound inches from my head and felt the slight breeze generated by the blindingly

rapid wing movements of a flying creature. A hummingbird was hovering directly over her face, perhaps six inches away, and it stayed there for what seemed like a surprisingly long time, well into the onset of her orgasmic mini convulsions. This was among the most extraordinary erotic experiences of my life. That lake is a transcendental spot in itself, and that visitation from such a stunning animal was such an aesthetic gift at such a sensually charged moment. I can't speak for her, but it was probably even more extraordinary for my partner since the intensely fluttering, brightly plumaged bird was hovering directly in front of her eyes the whole time, Sadly, while I would like to indulge in some mystical interpretation of the episode, it pains me to have to admit there is almost certainly a clear behavioral explanation for the bird's appearance: this friend is blond and very fair skinned, and she turns quite red when she gets excited. The hummingbird was undoubtedly checking out if this was a new strange red flower that might be a source of nectar, but I'm still deeply grateful to that small bird for helping provide me with such a sublime, exquisite erotic-aesthetic moment.

Animal Encounters

Felines

The Pregnant Mountain Lion in the Dark

I was staying with my then girlfriend at my favorite hot springs resort in Northern California (which I mentioned earlier in my section on deer), a place I have been going to for several days every year since 1977 to recuperate, meditate and practice t'ai chi intensely. We decided one night to go meditate in a place we really liked, a tiny, hidden waterfall tucked under the enormous root system of a stand of fig trees on a steep slope. The massive roots, which twist in wild patterns, seem to hold up the entire hillside, and the waterfall pours out of this tangled woody web. There is a short, easy path that leads to this spot, the only way in or out, other than doing some serious tree climbing and scrambling. There is a very small pool below the falls, and a flat area next to it with two chairs. A little Buddha statue sits up on a flat rock. I had often gone to meditate there during the heat of the day because it's shaded under the thick fig tree foliage, and the water keeps the temperature pleasantly cool. The sound of running water also really helps me clear my mind. It's an ideal little meditation nook. But I had never gone there at night.

We used small flashlights to find our way and then turned

them off after we sat down in the two chairs and began trying to meditate. It was absolutely pitch black, akin to an isolation tank. I was starting to get into a deeper state of focus when I heard a loud but very low both plaintive and menacing continuous growling sound that went on for maybe fifteen seconds. It seemed very, very close. I occasionally liked to make wolf or coyote-like howling or growling sounds either to fool around or when the urge hit me, but it seemed really unlikely that Rachel would pull such a stunt. She had a great sense of humor but this sort of gag would have been decidedly out of character, and I didn't think she (or most any other human) was capable of that sort of vocalization. She asked me in a whisper if I had made that sound. When I said I hadn't, it was obvious to both of us that there was a fairly large animal very close, behind us. We very slowly got up and tried to tiptoe away as unthreateningly as possible.

In the days following that incident I heard that a pregnant mountain lion had been sighted in the vicinity in the past week, and not long after our auditory encounter a hiker saw a mother lion with two young cubs fairly nearby. There are mountain lions in the region, but sightings are quite rare. When I tried to describe and mimic the sound we had heard for folks knowledgeable about the local fauna, they confirmed that this was almost certainly a mountain lion vocalization. The most likely scenario was that the mother lion was very close to giving birth and had found a den-like spot within the folds of those fig trees on the hillside that seemed hidden and safe to her, and that when we came and sat down feet away she waited for us to leave, but when we sat unmoving, it unnerved her, and she

expressed her angst and displeasure. We were very lucky that it was a lion in late pregnancy seeking solitude and not a hungry one seeking dinner, but I wonder if this lion, like the deer and wild turkeys that wander right among the humans in this community of new age hippie types, sensed that it might be safer giving birth among these atypical ahimsa-inspired primates than further out in the wild.

Animal Encounters

The Cannabis-Loving Kitten

In the early to mid 1970s I lived in a rundown, informally "communal" ten-bedroom, five-storey house with nine other people, all of us in our early twenties, in the Fort Greene section of Brooklyn. Most of us had been antiwar activists, but it was a transitional moment. The counterculture and radical political movements we had come out of were running out of steam, and we were mostly adrift, supporting ourselves as best we could as musicians, carpenters, cab drivers, social workers, teachers, nurses, and other means. Rent was cheap, fifty dollars each, but the heating bills in the winter were high due to the ancient dilapidated furnace and poor insulation. The old Italian boiler repairman who had come to check it out when we first moved in, said, when I asked him if we would survive the winter: "Ittsa gonna be rough; ittsa gonna be rough." He was prescient.

The neighborhood was quite mixed but predominantly working class African American. It had some middle class pockets, especially near Pratt, the art and design college some ten blocks away, but was far from crime free. A number of interracial couples had settled in the area in the previous few decades because it was diverse and tolerant compared to more monochromatic districts. Our block alone included Seventh Day Adventist families, moderately well known jazz musicians,

Felines

Thai transvestites, and Mexican mariachi enthusiasts (judging from the soundtrack of their loud parties). The area would soon begin a startling gentrification process (of which we were probably an early indicator), but it was still very funky.

There had been dozens and dozens of brothels there because of the proximity of the Brooklyn Navy Yard. During the war thousands of workers and soldiers had rented single rooms in brownstones converted to rooming houses and provided a large clientele for the prostitution trade. Apparently German agents had even operated a higher end brothel for navy officers in the neighborhood during the war in order to glean military and industrial intelligence. The prostitution business had gradually faded in the decades after the war, but the last four operating brothels were directly across the street from our house. The police ultimately cracked down on them with massive raids and a quasi-military occupation toward the end of our stay on that block.

Ironically perhaps, before those police raids, that house we all shared was in all likelihood the safest place I've ever lived. The pimps who ran the brothels did not want any street crime to disrupt business, and the houses they ran also rented out their extra rooms to a collection of older winos. This gaggle of totally harmless characters hung out on their stoops, but when the sun shone too brightly on their side of the street and it was shady on ours, or when they would be getting in the way of the hookers during prime business hours, they asked us if they could hang out on our stoop, and we readily acquiesced. This afforded us their affection, and nearly twenty-four-hour-a day-

vigilant protection and reliable intelligence about local affairs. No one could have broken into that house or have hassled us anywhere on that block.

Furthermore, many people in the area lived, at best, on the margins of legality. The garage next door to us, for example, often had cars come in one color and leave painted a radically different shade, with new plates. Everyone had too much to lose to poke around in anyone else's business. And this suited us fine, since, in that period of political paranoia, people we knew well had been involved in some deeply misguided violent actions and all their connections, including some of us, were being investigated assiduously. Those of us who had been the most aggressive activists were therefore highly fearful of the authorities, and we were all still immersed in the druggy counterculture of the era, so lying low in this neighborhood with its live-and-let-live, mind your own business vibe was ideal. Ironically, our immediate neighbors on one side, a very nice straight-laced matriarchal clan of black Seventh Day Adventists who had three children under ten, certainly viewed us as eccentric, but to them we were definitely a big improvement on the pimps or hookers, so they occasionally asked us to babysit their kids when they were in a pinch. We did so happily but we had to take every precaution to shield the kids from the sight of drugs and of far looser social mores in our house than they were accustomed to in theirs. We succeeded, but there were a few very close calls.

More than anyone else in our "commune," I sometimes had copious amounts of marijuana on hand. One of the women in

the house had adopted a couple of kittens, and though they were nominally hers, they wondered throughout the house, visiting whomever they chose. One of the two, named Shadow (though he was far greyer than black), always seemed to appear in my room when a fresh delivery of high quality marijuana appeared. The better the weed, the faster he'd show up. He also tended to avoid me when I was doing harder drugs, which, unfortunately, I indulged in too frequently in those fairly depressing years. Most cats are intuitively acute, but this one was especially highly attuned. This was one hip cat.

He didn't quite roll in the cannabis and flail wildly as some cats do when exposed to catnip, but he liked to sniff it and seemed to get very relaxed just being around it. He also really seemed to like reggae music, which I had gotten into heavily at the time, going deep into Crown Heights to the West Indian record stores to buy new 45s. Very few white people ventured into those neighborhoods then, and I was initially treated as though I were an undercover cop, until my affection for the music became well known, and I even began co-producing small reggae shows in a few Brooklyn and Manhattan clubs. Some of us met Bob Marley and some of the Wailers in those years, before they were international superstars, and followed them around to local gigs, but that's a whole other story.

Back to the cat: I really grew to love that little animal. I have never owned a cat or dog or any pet, but I've bonded with a number of them. I tend to be very responsible: if I take on a commitment, I want to be sure I can honor it. This makes me resistant to agreeing to anything that I have doubts about my

ability to see through impeccably. That probably explains my lifelong reluctance to make promises I'm not sure I can keep (e.g., marriage or Bodhisattva vows), as well as my fear to take on ownership of a pet. Urban, indoor life seems to me to be fundamentally incompatible with the nature of animals, even domesticated ones, but if one lets them roam in backyards, semi-feral cats kill millions of birds, and their risk of contracting lethal illnesses skyrockets as well. Furthermore, I travel extensively at times and am therefore absent for long stretches. I just couldn't ever guarantee the quality of life and well-being of a dependent animal when I haven't always been confident in my ability to guarantee mine, and in those years I really had doubts about how long my life was going to last, and whether prison or some other sorry fate awaited me. For this reason, when our communal house fell apart after a couple of years, I didn't make a push to adopt Shadow, and several others in the house had stronger claims to him than I did anyway. I was sad about it, but I saw him a few years later. He was in excellent care, but he had been spayed and had become a fat, lazy cat, no longer the slim, sophisticated bohemian he had been in his adolescence.

Women and Cats

Animal Encounters

Women and Cats

1. The Vengeful Siamese Cat

During the late 1970s I had an on-again/off-again bi-coastal relationship for a couple of years with a woman who lived in San Francisco. We usually only saw each other when she had time to take a vacation, and, generally, I would fly out west and we would go somewhere together from there, to places such as Hawaii or New Mexico or the Caribbean. She was ambitious in her career and worked very hard, and she tended to get sick for the first few days of nearly all these vacations, as it was the only time she would let herself rest and decompress. Due to the recuperative powers of a young body she always rebounded and we usually had a pretty good time, but what's more relevant to the theme of this text is that this young woman, who was quite leonine in her appearance and had many feline traits, also had a Siamese cat, a very jealous creature who deeply resented her mistress' absences, and this cat came to associate me, quite logically, with these departures.

I was at a stage in my life during which I was just beginning to emerge from a few years of sporadic hard drug use and trying to regain my health and vitality, starting to do yoga and t'ai chi, eating healthy food, and so on. I had consulted a naturopathic

doctor who had me on a rather elaborate vitamin and supplement regimen. Before going on trips, I would often organize all my vitamins, herbs and minerals in little piles before packing them into small plastic containers with daily doses. On one occasion I was engaged in this activity at my friend's apartment in San Francisco the night before our departure on one of these vacations. The cat watched me for a while and wandered off nonchalantly. Just when I was completely done dividing up all the piles, a very elaborate and time-consuming process, the cat suddenly appeared out of nowhere, quickly but casually leapt up onto the table I was working on and systematically batted all my little pills in every direction across the room. This was a perfectly planned and executed act of aggression, which my girlfriend thought was hysterically funny. With hindsight I of course see the humor in it, but I have to admit mirth wasn't my reaction at the time. My desires for retribution had to be quashed, as my girlfriend was far more attached to her cat than to me, and I was on her turf. I would soon discover she and the cat actually had a lot in common.

My friend was far less amused when her cat would take revenge upon her. This always happened after her return. This cat was very patient, and ruthlessly Machiavellian. She would never act out, by, say, tearing up clothes petulantly and randomly or moping about. She always picked a symbolic target my friend was deeply attached to, and very methodically defiled it in highly imaginative ways, and the damage was never obvious at first blush when re-entering the apartment. Everything would seem normal, but then my friend would scream hours or days later as she discovered that, say, her

favorite Chinese rug that had been stored in a closet was filled with cat feces, or that the favorite dress she only wore on rare occasions had been lacerated with mathematical precision. It was always only one target, and it was invariably damaged beyond full repair.

I was puzzled at the time that my friend tolerated this hyper jealous animal in her midst, but I now realize that she interpreted that possessiveness as a sign of love, and that she was in fact very comfortable with this type of power struggle in a relationship. I was totally out of my depth with this beautiful, smart, funny but fierce woman, capable of the harshest of scorpionic stings at the most vulnerable moments. This was someone highly versed in the war of the sexes, and I was so naïve at the time I didn't even realize I was in a war, so obviously the outcome of the engagement was never in doubt. I would have saved myself a couple of years of torment if I had been able to see right away that her familiar, that Siamese savant of revenge, was her mirror, and was actually the gentler of these two felines.

Women and Cats

2. The Psychic Cats

In my late 20s I was living alone in a fairly roomy duplex apartment in a brownstone in Fort Greene, and an ex girlfriend who was struggling and had lost her apartment asked me if she could use one of my extra rooms for a few months till she could save some money to get a new place. This was someone I had had a rather tempestuous breakup with a few years back and who was also a borderline alcoholic, but she was also one of the kindest and most warm-hearted people I have ever known, so I acquiesced. Her two cats moved in with her.

During the whole period she stayed with me, about four months, she had a very unpredictable schedule. She was looking for work some of the time, checking out potential living situations, going on occasional dates or outings with friends, and working several different part-time day and night gigs with frequently changing hours. It was usually impossible to predict when she would be leaving or coming back.

I worked at home, so I, unlike her, was in the apartment a lot of the time. One day a week or so after she moved in, she was out, and I was reading in my living room in the front of the building on the top floor facing the street, when I saw Jeannie's two cats suddenly, very atypically, race from her bedroom in the rear of the house, the whole length of the building, to the

window in the living room. They then both sat on the sill and stared intently, unmoving, up the street toward the corner. This house was some three blocks from the closest subway stop, roughly a three or four minute walk in that direction. I went up to the window and looked toward where the cats were staring and didn't see anything of interest. I was puzzled by their behavior, so I kept looking, and after about two minutes Jeannie appeared. The cats seemed to have sensed she was coming home, but their timing indicated they got this feeling as she was exiting the subway stop some three long blocks away.

Over the next four months I got to witness this ritual at least a dozen times at very different times of day and night, and the cats always reacted several minutes before Jeannie appeared on the corner. I never saw them act in that way when she wasn't coming. This was mostly during very cold months so the windows were closed, and there is no way they could have smelled her that far away with closed windows four stories up. There was also no sightline to the subway stop. One had to turn a corner to get there from our house, so there was no possible explanation involving one of the five senses for this behavior. I couldn't come up with any satisfactory explanation other than the fact that these cats just somehow always knew when their mistress was within a quarter mile or so, emerging from underground on her way home.

Women and Cats

3. The Death Throes of My Girlfriend's Cat

The longest amorous relationship I had lasted nearly a decade. I met the woman in question initially because she lived across the street from me. After we became involved, she eventually moved in to my house, after a year or two. She had a cat. I worked at home, and so I spent far more time with this cat than she did because she was off working most of each day.

Though it wasn't obvious when we first started living together, as she hadn't expressed that desire initially, one of the main bones of contention that emerged in our relationship after a while was that she really wanted to have a child and that I was not wildly enthusiastic about the idea. She was in her late-ish thirties by then, so it obviously made sense from a biological clock perspective. My main fear was that raising a child would be financially ruinous, and that I managed to keep myself afloat despite my relatively modest income only because I had of necessity become very frugal and disciplined in my financial life. She, on the other hand, earned far more than I did, but never seemed able to save any money and just seemed certain that there would always be enough money somehow. I've since discovered that fundamental differences in temperament regarding money are among the main sources of tension in couples and probably the cause of as many breakups as infidelity or alcohol.

Besides the financial fears, I also had the nagging suspicion

that, were we to have a child, I would wind up being the main one having to deal with parenting chores since I worked at home and had far more flexibility in my schedule. I did ultimately cooperate in her effort to get pregnant because the relationship did seem at its core like a really good one, definitely the most stable and serious I had ever had, and after all having children was something most people did. I was never wildly excited by the thought, but I didn't resist it either. I did what I was told regarding when to have sex; I went to get my sperm tested as instructed, etc., etc. I did insist that she prove to me she was capable of at least saving some money, just to meet me part of the way, but she consistently failed to do that. Those tensions over money eventually played a substantial role in breaking apart our relationship, but that breakup took place quite a few years in the future.

The attempt to have a child lasted a few years but ultimately failed despite her vigorous pursuit of the goal, probably due to medical impediments on her end, which may perhaps have been a good thing in that our relationship probably wouldn't have survived anyway, and we would have produced yet another kid growing up in shared custody, and I would have wound up far poorer than I am today, but it does make me sad for her because, cruelly, a large part of her work as a holistic healer involved fertility and pediatrics, and she was (and still is) very gifted at helping women get pregnant using natural means, something she became widely known for. That is just too painfully ironic. She obviously really wanted a child and would have been a great mother, I'm sure, and so I do feel a bit guilty that this woman lived with me during her last potentially fer-

tile years and failed to conceive. Perhaps if she'd been with a man who was more gung-ho about procreating the whole way through, she would have started attempting to get pregnant a few years earlier. Who knows?

All that said, back in those years when she first moved in with me and began, after a while, to express the desire to have a child, a crisis involving her cat highlighted and reinforced my fears. Her cat, with whom I had bonded simply because we were both around a lot of the time, began to express symptoms of some neurological ailment. Rather than a disease contracted by contagion such as distemper, this was almost certainly a genetic condition, because some close friends of my companion who lived a few blocks away had adopted a cat from the same litter, and that cat sibling got sick and died at exactly the same time in the same way.

As the cat got sicker and sicker, I wound up tending to it nearly all day for days on end, trying to comfort her as best I could, holding and stroking her, while my friend only had to deal with the situation after she got back from her long days at work. Finally, the disease progressed rapidly, and the cat began to go into prolonged shaking and convulsions for two days on end. I couldn't believe how long this was lasting and how much suffering the poor animal was enduring. My friend finally realized that nothing more could be done and that she had to take the cat to the vet to be put down, but when she came home early to deal with the situation and tried to soothe the cat and hold her, it scratched and bit her: it rejected her, while it let me hold her. The cat was expressing in her final acts her feelings of neg-

lect and abandonment to her owner. My friend couldn't really accept that and chose to interpret the cat's behavior as somehow the result of an incoherent mental state the illness must have induced, and I kept silent, but I had come to know that cat quite well, and I understood its actions and its intent perfectly clearly. It may have been in agony and on death's door, but it was totally lucid.

My friend was of course sobbing as she took the cat to the vet, and was heartbroken when she came home, so I had to comfort her and play the role of the strong, supportive partner, when the truth was that I was totally traumatized from having had, all by myself, all day long every day for a couple of weeks, been trying to comfort a dying animal in great pain. And I had never chosen to have a cat. One reason I have never had pets is that I really didn't want to live through situations like that, but this one had been imposed on me, and my temperament made it impossible for me to ignore the pain of a living creature. And then of course my friend was the one who had the privilege of wallowing in righteous sorrow and to be comforted by one and all, because it was "her" cat. The lessons to be drawn about how child rearing would most likely have taken place in our household were not lost on me.

Women and Cats

Animal Encounters

Canids

Coyotes

I have never had any encounters with wolves other than seeing them in captivity in zoos or similar contexts or on wildlife programs on television, so the only direct experiences I have had with wild canids are with coyotes. I had always associated coyotes with the Western states. My first awareness of the existence of this species in childhood came from the Road Runner cartoons that featured exotic desert landscapes, and later from Native American mythologies from what I imagined was "out west" somewhere. And, in fact, for a long time most of my experiences of coyotes were in the western U.S.

I had friends in Topanga Canyon, and I remember visiting them back in the 1970s and eating on the nice outdoor terrace of a fancy health food restaurant there run by an esoteric religious cult (that later in the 1980s built elaborate bunkers and bomb shelters in Montana in preparation for the apocalypse) and seeing the coyotes just on the other side of the dry creek bed, staring attentively at us as we chewed our food. Coyotes have long been all over suburban Los Angeles and on occasion poach people's pets. In more recent years a few have even established themselves in San Francisco's Golden Gate Park.

Canids

What was surprising about those particular coyotes watching us eat in Topanga was that they made no efforts to hide, while coyotes generally tend to be extremely discreet and furtive.

I have run into a couple of coyotes while backpacking. In Wyoming's Wind River Range in a fairly remote area with few other humans around, I was hiking along a trail when what I thought was someone's skinny German Shepherd came ambling toward me on the trail, with, I assumed, its owners not far behind. The "dog" then stopped in its tracks and looked up and saw me (it had been looking down and to the sides, probably for voles or other small animals to eat) and froze in its tracks, quite comically, then bolted manically into the underbrush. It actually felt for a moment like a real life re-enactment of a Road Runner cartoon.

My closest encounter occurred when I was on a car trip in northern New Mexico and stopped to sleep in a minimalistic campsite along a rural road. The weather was warm and clear, so I had just plunked my sleeping bag down on the ground. In the middle of the night I woke up, and a coyote was looking right into my eyes from just off to my left no more than 2 feet away. At first, I once again assumed it must be someone's dog (had I been more alertly awake, I would have immediately realized it had no collar), so I wasn't startled and didn't jump up. It too seemed calm and just stared at me for a moment and then ambled off. As it left I recognized the characteristic loping stride, long muzzle and body shape of a coyote, and there were no other people around, so it obviously wasn't anyone's dog. I wondered why it had been staring at me from so close. I

have to assume it wasn't going to chomp on my face. It may have been sniffing around to see if I had stashed any food nearby, but I had to admire its chutzpah, sneaking up so close to a fairly big sleeping primate, and one from the planet's most murderous species that had certainly slaughtered far more of its brethren than all other animals combined.

In the last couple of decades, coyotes, unheard of in New England and New York forests during most of my life, have spread throughout the East Coast and are now well established throughout the region. Wolves probably kept them out for millennia, but the extermination of wolves in most of the East by the end of the 19th Century opened a door for them, and in fact Eastern coyotes have taken over part of the wolf's former ecological niche. They are much bigger than their Western cousins and hunt bigger game such as deer far more frequently. At least some of them are almost certainly wolf/coyote hybrids.

These extraordinarily opportunistic and clever animals are now establishing themselves in large Eastern cities. When one first made it through all the dense exurbs and suburbs and the immense gritty urban landscapes of the Bronx to get to Central Park in 2006, it stunned the city, but in 2010 a coyote led the cops on a wild chase through lower Manhattan before being finally trapped in a parking lot in TriBeCa, and now a number of coyotes have wandered into the city over the years. At least four others were sighted in 2010 alone, in Harlem, near Columbia University and in Central Park, and they're now seen in Chicago and Boston. The odds are that some

small populations have already or will soon establish themselves in niches even in these urban cores and keep spreading east and south to colonize the entire country.

This "re-wilding" of the East Coast forests as exemplified by the resuscitation of eagle and hawk populations, the return of plentiful flocks of wild turkeys, the spread of moose, even occasional sightings of cougars, and other indicators, is one of the most hopeful environmental stories on the planet in that one of the most densely populated urban corridors on Earth seems capable of co-existing with re-wooded landscapes and growing populations of large mammals and predators.

Part of this success story is an accidental one. Colonial era farmers had largely denuded the northeastern forests, but when far better agricultural lands opened up in the Midwest in the second half of the 19th Century, the settlers abandoned most of the Northeast's farms, and second and third growth forests slowly re-conquered the rocky soils of New England and the mid Atlantic on their own. The rise of eco-awareness starting in the late 1800s accompanied by at least some radically improved environmental stewardship in recent decades has also made an enormous difference. There are still very real threats, especially the ravages climate change is already starting to bring to many tree species, and the never-ending pressures of growing populations and overdevelopment, but it's one of the few large ecosystems on Earth that is far healthier now that it was a century ago. Some of us dream of well established wildlife corridors that would connect the big chunks of wild lands in the Northeast: the Laurentians in Quebec;

the Adirondacks, Catskills and Shawangunks in New York State; the Green Mountains in Vermont and Whites in New Hampshire; Baxter State Park and the Allagash wilderness of northern Maine; the Alleghenies in Pennsylvania; the Ramapos and Pine Barrens and New Jersey highlands; etc., to create a truly vibrant web of connected woodland ecosystems alongside the network of megacities that characterize our region.

Coyotes are an early indicator of that possibility. They could perhaps play the opposite role that young artists and bohemians do when they serve as the advance guard of gentrification in gritty urban neighborhoods. Coyotes seem, here in the East, to be the vanguard of re-wilding. They are the predators most capable of spreading across even very challenging urbanized landscapes to establish themselves wherever sufficient food and cover exist because they are so adaptable, omnivorous, sly and furtive. Their stealth is what surprises me the most about them. During the portions of the many summers I spent in the Catskill Mountains over the decades, I saw the arrival and then the firm establishment of coyotes throughout the region.

Or, actually, I didn't see it; I heard it. I really enjoy sitting out on a porch in the country in the dark in the still of the night and tend to do it every night when I have the chance, and the howls of coyote packs slowly began to become more common over the years until they were ubiquitous and a nightly occurrence. In fact those howls became the dominant feature of the nocturnal soundscape, but I almost never saw any actual animals. I saw a lone coyote on only two occasions over decades

of hiking fairly often in those mountains. These are creatures of paradox: they are not at all shy about making a lot of noise, and there are a whole lot of them all around these days, but they are really, really good at staying out of sight.

Animal Encounters

Dogs

Like just about everyone in our society, I've had my share of experiences with dogs. I've never, as I mentioned, ever owned one, but I've had temporary custody of a few, been not infrequently called upon to walk a number of them, befriended a few that belonged to friends or neighbors, and had run-ins with feral dogs. Most of these short-term relationships have been very pleasant, but a few of my most vivid memories of dogs are of frightening episodes.

The most terrifying incident occurred when I was perhaps 6 or 7 years old, while we were visiting some friends of my parents who lived in Westchester County. The adults went outside for some reason, and I was left to play in the living room of this big country house. These people had a Doberman, and this dog had been left in the house with me. For some reason, it must have perceived me as an alien presence or just didn't like children, and it began to snarl and bark at me very loudly, baring its formidable teeth and spewing spittle and foam out of its mouth. It herded me up against a wall and kept up its very intense display of ferocious aggression less than a foot or two away from me. I was far too scared to move, which was probably a very good thing as whenever I twitched even slightly its body language made it clear that it was ready to tear into me should I move more than an iota. This lasted what seemed like

Canids

an eternity until the adults returned and calmed the dog down. I was sobbing and totally traumatized. I don't remember if I pissed in my pants, but it wouldn't surprise me if I had. The most intense of our childhood terrors stay with us forever, I think.

On two separate occasions many years later I stupidly tried to break up a really intense dog fight between two male dogs and got some pretty bad bites for my efforts. On a few other occasions while strolling or jogging in unfamiliar rural or suburban areas I got chased by packs of dogs, some just gangs of local pets, others semi-feral or fully feral dogs, and while those episodes resulted in intense sprints and definitely raised my heartbeat, none of them ever rose to the same level of terror as that childhood episode with the Doberman.

Speaking of Dobermans, I noticed over the decades here in Brooklyn fads among a certain set of dog owners who seek out the most ferocious breeds they can. For a few years in the 70s and early 80s, it was Dobermans that were the most prized. Later pit bulls became the favored breed. It was clear that some of these dogs were being trained to take part in canine combat. I would see very macho guys training their Dobermans and later pit bulls in Fort Greene Park. One guy would force his dog to hang from a branch by his teeth for a really long time and not let go until his owner gave him the order, and he would beat the dog if it let go prematurely. That neighborhood was quite a bit wilder then. I also not infrequently found decapitated roosters from Santeria rituals. I suspect gentrification has probably curtailed at least some of

those nocturnal activities. While I still see the occasional tough looking dude with a pit bull or two, the more prevalent sorts of canine fads in my part of Brooklyn these days involve fashionably attired young women wearing sunglasses carrying various breeds of hideous looking, rodent-sized dogs in their purses.

But, as I said, most of my experiences with dogs have been far more pleasant. That same very sweet older rich heiress friend of my parents' at whose Long Island estate I was taken on that traumatic squirrel hunting expedition, owned a delightfully lovable female golden retriever named Cassandra, and during my childhood, when we spent the occasional long weekend at this woman's property (a small island called Duck Island near the town of Huntington), I would spend hours racing through the woods and marshes of this large private estate accompanied by this tirelessly playful animal. I've never had as ideal a play companion, and though I only spent a few days of my life with her in toto, and the last time was far more than 50 years ago, my romps with Cassandra provided me with some of the most idyllic memories of my childhood.

There is something about dogs' instincts for pack behavior that must awaken thrilling archaic memories from the collective unconscious about our own ancestors' pack hunting adventures. It also helps that dogs will very often accept a human as the automatic alpha pack leader, and the few times I have been accompanied by several dogs on a hike in wild lands, it has given me quite a thrill. I used to visit some friends in the 1970s after they moved to the Chimayo Valley in northern New Mexico, and at one point they had four dogs. On several occa-

sions I went on hikes with this whole canine crew, and I was amazed how they deferred to me as the group leader even though they knew the terrain and I didn't, and one of them was a big, strong, feisty male who had on a few occasions wandered off many dozens of miles away. At one point, as it was very hot and the sun was very bright in this high desert landscape, I stopped under a small scrubby piñon tree to rest in the shade, and the four dogs, who all obviously wanted to keep moving, all stopped and waited patiently, huddling under whatever tiny bits of shade they could find next to cacti, bushes, or small junipers, and only began walking again when I got up and started moving. They were going to await my orders no matter how antsy they were, and these dogs had only just met me. I have to admit this feeling of having the loyal obedience of a whole troupe of big, vigorous animals, was quite a rush. I've never had as visceral a sense of power, though whenever I've seen professional dog walkers with much bigger packs of dogs, they've always seemed more harried than empowered. I guess trying to control a bunch of leashed, neurotic, urban animals who spend the great majority of their lives in small apartments must not be quite the same as leading a pack of robust country dogs through the wilds.

The capacity of certain dogs to focus obsessively on a very specific play or athletic activity is something I've always been amazed by. During the last few years, some of my best and oldest friends with whom I stay on my annual trips to San Francisco, Adam and Adelina, have had a young, incredibly fit dog, a German Shepherd/Rottweiler mix named Mocha, and I've taken her to the nearby beach on quite a few occasions to

engage in her favorite activity—retrieving a thrown tennis ball. My friends have a tool that's very popular among dog owners, a "Chuck-It," a long plastic dog toy a little bit reminiscent of a jai alai *xistera* that permits one to throw a ball much farther than if one were just using one's arm motion. No matter how often I throw the ball down the beach as far as I can using this device, and I've tried on multiple occasions to exhaust the dog by throwing the ball over and over again, I've only managed to exhaust myself, and I'm fairly fit. Her running speed never flags. She sprints at top speed every single time. She is so single-minded that she ignores all distractions—other dogs, people, birds, or anything else. Her entire attention is taken by the chase after and retrieval of the ball. I get the impression she would run herself to death. This may seem obsessive to us humans, but I can't help but admire the absolute commitment to a game, the extreme one-pointedness of a behavior that seems to land somewhere between pathology and enlightenment.

Speaking of canine enlightenment, back in 1969/1970 one of the collectives/communes that was part of the landscape of the local radical left "movement" back then in the city and with whom I hung out on occasion, had two part German Shepherd/part mutt dogs. Now this collective was a bit of a ragged crew. They had two main leaders who were daring, macho types who had pulled off a few impressive actions, but both those guys were a bit nuts. One, the black sheep of an Irish family of cops—his father, all his siblings and cousins—had become famous for climbing a tree his college wanted to cut down on the center of the campus and refusing to come

down for days till the police had to be called in to climb way up and pull him down. This of course has become a well-known tactic in recent years in environmental actions, but it was highly unusual then, especially in NYC. This guy was very well read in political theory for someone coming from such a blue-collar (literally) background, but he was relentlessly fanatical, in a way that stuck out even for a milieu in which fanaticism was de rigueur. The other one was a really tough guy who carried guns and was getting more and more into the cannabis economy and personal hard drug use.

The ten or so core members of this group lived in a couple of adjoining apartments on a run-down block on the Upper West Side, and they had knocked down the wall between the units without asking the landlord's permission, and I'm not talking about a construction project: they just took a sledge-hammer to the wall till they could move from one apartment to the other well enough. Loose bricks still littered the floor. There were political slogans crudely spray-painted on the walls. The place was truly squalid, and there were always a lot of drugs around, though that was true just about everywhere I frequented back then.

The two dogs may have been the sanest members of this crew. I took them out to the park on a few occasions. One of the two seemed especially extremely intelligent, resourceful and centered, like an old soul. She never seemed puzzled or anxious and when she looked into your eyes, you really got the sense that she could understand you perfectly clearly and maybe knew more than you did about all kinds of things. She could

Animal Encounters

convey that she was hungry or thirsty in a way that seemed almost telepathic. You could leave her off the leash in the park, and she would wander far and even disappear from sight for a while, but she never failed to return just when you were ready to go back, as though she could read your mind at a distance, and she always made sure the other dog, her male sibling, came back too. She didn't seem afraid of anything, but she never got in trouble with other dogs or people. Now the story about this dog was that, according to the members of this wild household, someone had left some forty hits of blotter acid (i.e. for the non former hippies among you: pure LSD doses soaked onto a sheet of paper) on a low table or the floor, perhaps near some food scraps (certainly possible in their chaotic apartment), and that the dog had wound up ingesting the whole sheet of paper, but had not manifested any noticeably bizarre symptoms, and, if anything, had seemed to them smarter and sharper since the incident. Now I have no idea whether this actually happened or if it was just part of their collective mythology, an urban legend. These folks back at that time could just as easily have misplaced large amounts of drugs and imagined the dog ate them, but they were all firmly convinced of the veracity of the tale. In any case, that was definitely one exceptional dog.

Canids

The Feral Dog at my Door

One day in the mid 1980s I was running late for what seemed at the time like an important appointment in Manhattan. In a hurry, I began to come out the front door of my Fort Greene, Brooklyn brownstone at a rapid clip, eager to get to the subway at Atlantic Avenue, hoping to get lucky and catch a train right away, but there, right in front of my door was the most ragged feral dog I had ever seen. For some reason this dog had picked my house, which was smack-dab in the middle of the block, and had actually climbed to the top of my stoop (and these brownstone stoops are one-storey high).

At first I was a bit scared that the dog might have rabies or, even if it didn't, that it would bite me, as it bared its teeth and snarled at me as I came out, so I retreated back into my doorway, keeping the door slightly ajar. This animal looked truly pathetic. Its hair had mostly fallen out, with only a few patches remaining; it had scars all over; it was nearly all bone; it had some missing teeth, and its gums were in terrible shape. This dog had been on its own for a very long time, perhaps its whole life. I had never seen that sickly and pathetic looking a canine, or any creature.

We looked at each other for a minute or so, and I realized that this animal was not rabid, and I had the feeling that it wasn't going to bite me if I didn't provoke it, so I came out my door.

Animal Encounters

We were facing each other on top of the stoop. I tried to get closer, but it snarled. There was no way this dog was going to let a human being touch it after a life of trauma. It really didn't look as though this animal had any chance of surviving very long. It seemed to nearly certainly be at death's door. It was almost a miracle it was still alive. I could have just gone to the subway and on to my engagement, but somehow I couldn't just leave it there.

This was a period in my life during which I had been doing an enormous amount of reading on spiritual and esoteric topics and had been trying to "work" fairly assiduously on my psycho-spiritual development, so I had been wrestling with a lot of moral issues. I'm not sure if this ultimately affected the way I handled the situation, in that my core temperament may have ultimately led me to the same choices even without any of that attempt at spiritual cultivation, but it certainly made the ethical conundrums this situation presented seem more significant and intense.

Did I have a responsibility toward this probably about-to-die fellow creature in great pain? I didn't feel I could take it in or care for it, as it wouldn't let me touch it or guide it, and I had tenants and roommates in the house who would freak out, and whose safety I felt responsible for, plus, to be honest, I really didn't want to bring it into my house either, and I still felt I had to get to my engagement, but was there a reason it picked my house and me? Was this some sort of lesson or test?

I was really eager to get to my appointment, but I just couldn't leave the dog there without doing something. I decided that at

the very least it deserved a last meal, but I was mostly vegetarian and had nothing in the house that a dog would eat. Also I was very familiar with Taoist and other teaching stories about the unintended consequences of actions and the risks of trying to "do good." "The road to hell is paved with good intentions" had, in fact, been one of my father's favorite sayings. If I fed this dog so that it was re-invigorated enough to begin roaming the streets for a while longer, might it bite a child or endanger people or other dogs, and might that just be prolonging its miserable life a tiny bit longer anyway? Maybe the most humane and safest thing to do was just to shoot it, but that was not something I was capable of and there were far too many logistical and legal problems with that course of action.

Another strange aspect of the episode was that there didn't seem to be anyone at all around on my block. It was the middle of the day, and there would nearly always be people walking by or parking their cars or getting in or out of their houses at that time of day, but I was the only human being around. In hindsight, I realized that it had never occurred to me to call animal control authorities or the police. In any case, that would have taken a long time, as this was before cellphones, and in those days city bureaucracies were even far less efficient than they are today. It also probably never occurred to me because the anarchist leanings of my youth still colored my worldview, so I usually balked at involving the authorities or the gendarmerie in any situation unless a real emergency called for it.

I decided that I should treat this dog the way I would hope to

be treated were I in its paws, with its current mindset. So I walked quickly down the street, one block down to a butcher store on Lafayette Avenue. I bought a bunch of ground beef and came back. It took a few minutes, but the dog was still there, at the top of my stoop. I climbed back up and put the ground beef down in front of it. It didn't go for the meat right away, as it was still very skittish and was afraid to eat with a person standing so close. I left it there and went into the city, hoping to still salvage something from the appointment, which seemed really important at the time, but the nature of which I, of course, have totally forgotten, while the memory of that dog has stayed vividly etched in my memory over the decades.

When I got back several hours later, the dog was gone; the wax paper that the beef had been wrapped in was there, but the meat had all been eaten and the paper licked clean. To this day I have no idea if I did the right thing, though I lean toward feeling that my choice was a valid one. I hadn't been saintly enough to take it in, but this animal, it seemed to me, deserved at least one small kind gesture, a fleeting moment of pleasure and relief in its sad life, even if that reprieve was almost certainly very brief.

Canids

Panda

One of my best friends from college, Ray, an extremely unconventional person back then, also turned out to have a radically unorthodox attitude to dog ownership back in his younger days. Ray had multi-faceted pursuits: he had run track; played competitive chess; been a professional photographer (including for the band "Sly and the Family Stone"); was a radical activist on campus; had keen interests in music and film, etc. He didn't always stick with each pursuit, but he made many friends and connections in all these separate universes. I think he knew (and still knows) more people than anyone on the planet, including politicians and public relations superstars. This web of connections would later turn out to come in very handy when it came to his dog.

Ray was somewhere around the middle of the pack of the offspring in a working-class black family in Watts, in Los Angeles, which in the 1960s was a hotbed of racial tension and police repression, but that challenging environment never limited Ray. Perhaps because his family was stable and supportive and because he had such a sharp mind, Ray always seemed to feel the entire world was his oyster, full of wonderful games and enterprises one could engage in. He was playful and fearless. I don't think it ever occurred to him that he couldn't do whatever he wanted anywhere. He got a small motorbike when still a

young teenager and cruised all over wide swaths of California in the wild mid 60s, even though the police stopped him constantly for "driving while black" (and young). He was always curious and restless and ready to check things out. He was far from naïve, but he was relentlessly positive in his outlook, as free of malice as anyone I've ever met, and able to talk and charm himself out of all sorts of potentially dangerous situations again and again (and back in those days, a number of us tended to wind up in scary episodes with alarming frequency).

Ray had brought his restlessness and wanderlust with him to the East Coast when he got a scholarship to Columbia, where I met him. This was the late 1960s/early 1970s, a highly charged political and cultural period, and Columbia was one of the epicenters of all this ferment, and Ray was fully engaged with all of it, but, very much unlike most undergraduates he also roamed the whole city, cultivating his highly varied interests and immersing himself in many very different milieus. One result of this was that he was always on the go, and often moved, living in many different apartments, and meeting countless people all over the place.

At one point, Ray got a puppy, part Border-Collie, part Australian Shepherd, with some German Wirehaired Pointer thrown in, who quickly grew into a big, very distinctive mostly black animal with prominent white patches, fittingly named Panda Bear, Panda for short. Panda had come from a litter that belonged to a very hip New York couple. The woman was an Andy Warhol starlet and the guy was the leader of a rock group that was for a while the main band of the radical move-

ment in the city, that played all the benefits and that had its Warholian fifteen minutes of fame in the larger culture when they backed John Lennon and Yoko for a while.

Ray never leashed his dog. He insisted on Panda learning to follow him around as he raced around the city. Early on Panda had a few close calls and got mild injuries from getting hit by cars a couple of times, but by and large seemed to have mastered street life after six months or so. Ray loved his dog but did not coddle him. Panda had to learn to navigate the urban jungle. He ultimately became as street-wise and tough as any dog could be and developed his own agenda. He learned how to do his own cruising and bopping, keeping just enough of an eye on Ray so he could race and catch up when needed. And Ray would sometimes go to a movie or show or to a social engagement to which he couldn't bring a dog, and he would just leave the dog, untied, outside, and tell him to wait, sometimes for hours. Amazingly, most of the time Panda was there when Ray returned, though occasionally he had wandered off and we had to yell his name a while and look around before he would finally turn up. Ray also left Panda with a wide range of friends for different periods of time. I took care of him for several weeks on a couple of occasions, but I was one of many, so this dog was used to hanging out with a wide array of people.

On a few occasions over the years Ray lost his dog. He had left him outside some film or play or venue, as was his habit, but when he came out of where he had been, in these instances Panda was completely gone. This happened a handful of times, and in each case it later turned out that someone had

come upon this big, cute, friendly dog and assumed he was abandoned since he was untied (and in those days, didn't have a collar either!) and had taken him home, and Panda, probably curious and open to trying new things, like his owner, and totally accustomed to living among many humans, went along willingly. The longest of these episodes lasted some six months, but each time someone who knew Ray would eventually spot Panda on the street and inform the new owners that this dog belonged to someone they knew, and Panda and Ray would be reunited. Usually the people were happy to return him, as Panda wasn't used to being leashed. Ray's extraordinarily extensive networks of friends and acquaintances covered all of Manhattan and not insignificant swaths of the other boroughs as well, so someone he knew was bound to spot his very distinctive dog before too much time passed.

Eventually Ray settled into a more stable, long-term residence in the tucked-away Vinegar Hill neighborhood of waterfront Brooklyn, still fairly desolate and sparsely populated in those years, and Panda, who wandered the neighborhood at will, became the top dog, the godfather, the reigning canine monarch of this slowly gentrifying but gritty, hidden neighborhood, fathering many offspring. He lived to be eighteen. To this day one can occasionally spot some of his descendants, very distinctively Panda Bear-like black and white dogs around Vinegar Hill and into the adjoining Dumbo neighborhood as well. Panda, more than any urban dog I've ever known, straddled the boundary between a semi-feral state and domestication, and may have ultimately interacted with more fascinating people at all ends of the socio-economic spectrum than any

member of his species. Panda's trajectory perfectly reflected the spirit of the city in those years. He was the ultimate New York of the 1970s and 80s dog.

Animal Encounters

Primates

Homo Sapiens sapiens

I have had very little experience with non-human primates. I've never been to Africa or Asia, so my only experience of most monkeys or great apes has come from TV wildlife shows or zoos. I have seen a few troupes of howler monkeys in the jungles of Central America. The ones that seemed to guard the entrance to the Mayan ruins at Tikal in Guatemala were particularly feisty and aggressive when I visited that site, making a huge racket and throwing small branches down from the treetops in our general direction. I've seen captive pet spider monkeys in various parts of Mexico and Guatemala who seemed cute initially but could become very annoying very quickly as they grabbed my hair and scratched and bit me, but to their defense, they seemed very badly treated by their owners. In the Peruvian Amazon I heard some howler monkeys a few nights in the distance, but sadly, most of the places I stayed in the jungle seemed to have been overly hunted, so the wildlife there was scarce.

So my only real exposure to primates has been to my own species, Homo sapiens sapiens. I realize that including episodes about humans may perhaps seem like cheating in a collection that is entitled "Animal Encounters," but, hey, we too are ani-

Primates

mals, extremely complicated and kinky animals, but animals nonetheless, so it felt appropriate to me to at least include a couple of anecdotes involving our branch of the primate family. I have, like nearly any human being, had far too many encounters and experiences with other members of my species to ever hope to describe even a tiny percentage of them, so I have only included two stories about Homo sapiens here, each dealing with very specific themes.

Animal Encounters

The Flute Player

I met him in Prospect Park. I had long been going most late afternoons to a specific spot toward the center of the "Great Meadow" in that park to do calisthenics, stretch, and mostly to practice t'ai chi. I had at one time sought out more isolated, remote parts of the park, but once in a while young men who had obviously watched too many kung fu films would come by and challenge me in combat. I decided I needed to find a spot which was in a more populated part of the park but that still afforded enough space, so that I could maintain a good distance from other people to be able to focus and practice without disturbance. This spot fit the bill and was nicely shielded from wind as it was in a slight dip in the terrain. It was in a favorite area for a subculture of serious kite flyers, but their activity didn't generally impede mine, except on rare occasions when a kite would crash near me, and the kite-flyers tolerated my presence.

When I practice, I try to project enough of a mildly intimidating aura so that people will give me a wide berth and not plunk themselves down too close, and it usually works, as I'm very good at giving annoying people a scowl and the "hairy eyeball." That said, the unwritten rules about giving strangers sufficient space and minding your own business that I grew up

with as a native New Yorker seem to have eroded with newer residents who don't seem to know the rules of tolerable proximity or that engaging in loud phone conversations just meters away is a form of aggression.

There are more and more of these people, and it feels deeply disconcerting not to feel at home in one's native city because the unspoken codes of conduct, the basic rules of body language, street etiquette and personal space no longer seem to apply. So, I sometimes have to try to appear even more intimidating when too many of these ever more numerous solipsistic narcissists are afoot. Anyway, all that to explain that, in general, other than children, who are naturally curious and dogs who want to play, both of whom I happily engage with, as well as the occasional serious martial artist who wants to compare notes and knows the proper protocols of respectful approach, I see to it that people leave me alone when I go to the park to practice.

During a period of a few weeks one springtime a guy frequently showed up in that part of the park at the same time as I was there and sat up on a rise some 40 or so yards away and played a Japanese bamboo flute. He kept his distance, seemed like a serious guy doing his thing, and though he didn't seem like a master flutist, his music had a deep soulful quality and was great accompaniment for what I was doing, so I was happy he was there, but we didn't make any effort to converse. We were each engaged in our own practice.

Animal Encounters

Eventually, after a few weeks, I don't remember how it came about, but we had become accustomed to each other's presence, and we started to chat. I told him I enjoyed his playing and asked him if it was a Shakuhachi flute. I remembered an album of Shakuhachi flute called *Music for Zen Meditation* that had been in every hip cat's pad (including mine) during my younger years and that was my main association with Japanese bamboo flutes. To be honest, it was the only Japanese bamboo flute I knew the name of, but he told me that he was actually playing a different type of bamboo flute, a Hocchiku flute. The guy, probably in his mid fifties, seemed very centered, with the luminous eyes of someone who had done some serious exploration of consciousness and had thought deeply about life. He seemed totally unpretentious and very present. He impressed me as a man of real substance. He told me he admired my focus and dedication to t'ai chi and enjoyed playing while I practiced. Then we each went back to doing our own thing, and we would wave and nod to each other respectfully from a distance after that when we were both around at the same time.

A few weeks went by and we wound up talking again, and I began to ask him about himself. He had terminal cancer he said. He had been told he had only a few months to live. I pressed him because he seemed so vital, but he said he had tried every approach both allopathic and alternative that he could in the previous few years, and that there was, realistically, nothing left to do.

Primates

I saw him once or twice after that, but then he was no longer around. I never knew his name, but I still sometimes hear the sound of that Hocchiku flute in my mind when I walk by his spot all these years later.

Animal Encounters

The Perfect Couple

I met R and L at the "new age" hot springs resort in northern California that I've described previously sometime around the mid 1980s. I saw L doing t'ai chi on one of the decks there, and while she wasn't a high level practitioner, her form wasn't bad at all. It had structural integrity and elegance. A lot of people at this resort practiced yoga, but in those days, I had seen very few people practicing t'ai chi or any Chinese martial arts or related disciplines there, and, to be honest, the fact that she was an attractive woman also helped spark my interest. When she was done with her form and was about to wander off, I went up and said hello and asked her where she had learned t'ai chi and so on. It turned out that she had studied in New York at a school I was familiar with, and in fact lived in New York with her husband, R, who was also at the hot springs, and whom she introduced me to a few minutes later.

We hung out that afternoon for a few hours and shared our contact information back home. I really enjoyed their company. They were very fit looking, radiant types with bright, luminous eyes and glowing skin, and were into very healthy lifestyles and spiritual pursuits, but they weren't at all silly New Age types. They were sharp and funny and had a New York Jewish edge with a healthy dose of sardonic humor, which I find extremely appealing.

Primates

I got in touch with them a while after I got back home, and I began to get to know them. They were both practitioners of different types of bodywork: L did Swedish massage and Shiatsu and R practiced a more esoteric technique called Cranio-sacral therapy. They were both very skilled at their work, had many clients, and they were very well connected in the "alternative" health and spirituality scene in the city, which was quite a bit smaller then than now. They were a sort of a mini power couple in some of these small universes and would occasionally organize events or parties that brought quite a few of the leading lights of these subcultures together.

Their apartment was always spotlessly clean and never cluttered, a sort of Zen Danish-modern look, with very bright, impeccable white paint on the walls. There were many houseplants strategically spaced to purify the air with optimal efficiency and a whole wall of trays of the wheat grass and the various sprouts they grew in abundance. They seemed to me to be an archetypal model of perfection: always in vibrant health and in good spirits, never seeming to have serious disagreements, and yet feisty and highly intelligent. One could have lively conversations with each of them separately. There didn't seem to me to be any unhealthy power imbalance between them. They both practiced yoga assiduously, etc.

Now, in my own circle of friends, I was viewed as a health nut. I exercised vigorously, ate a mostly vegetarian, organic diet, meditated, etc., but I felt like a complete slacker compared to these two. I kept late hours; they were up at the crack of dawn. I drank coffee; green tea was the strongest stimulant they ever

consumed. I was frequently plagued with doubts about many things and often ambivalent or unsure about which path to follow; they seemed absolutely sure of themselves, with clear goals and targets.

Part of me was suspicious of this image of perfection, but I couldn't see any symptoms of hidden dysfunction, so I was for the most part impressed, even awed by them. They had a sort of a multi-year plan, which involved having a child, saving a certain amount of money and then moving to Los Angeles, where R had close family and personal history and a solid web of movie business connections. R had been working on screenplays, and was absolutely certain that with his contacts and the quality of his work, he was going to be successful in that world and they would live in one of LA's nicer canyons.

I tend to be incredibly skeptical of people with absolute certainty about their beliefs or worldviews, and even more so of those who are supremely confident their personal plans will come to pass exactly as they foresee. My experience of the world is that it is often a very unpredictable place, and while I hope my plans succeed, I never expect them to without at least some extremely convoluted bifurcations, and am never totally surprised when things turn out quite differently than anticipated. But I have over the course of my life met a few people who seemed so confident in their destiny, and were charismatic enough, smart enough, and convincing enough that I suspended most of my disbelief and figured that, OK, maybe this person really can pull this off. And of course one hears stories about this or that famous person who knew he/she was going

Primates

to "make it" to stardom in this or that domain from a tender age, and so one has to admit that it does, at least on rare occasions occur.

Cleary there is something about confidence most people find powerfully seductive. A charismatic figure with absolute certainty about this or that ideology will almost invariably attract some followers. Still, that type of certainty about future plans always makes me very uncomfortable. It makes me feel like an insecure "Doubting Thomas" in comparison to the paragon of confidence standing before me, and it challenges my fundamental view of how the universe operates. I tend to believe that anything or anyone too bright, too perfect, must harbor a big dark shadow, but then I feel guilty because I wonder if by harboring doubts about this person's odds of success I am secretly hoping he/she fails, because that quality of one-pointedness and focus makes me feel so flawed and inferior.

Though nearly all the people I had met who exuded that sort of confidence had not ultimately succeeded in their aspirations, I had also seen a couple of people who seemed like real basket cases ultimately succeed beyond my wildest expectations, so I felt I had to stay open-minded, especially since I was only in my 30s at that point, and I hadn't witnessed sufficient long arks of life trajectories first hand. If anybody could achieve their dreams, these two seemed like the ones.

And R and L's lives in those years really did conform to their plan. They had an adorable baby girl, as cute and healthy as one would expect with such parents, and after exactly the number of years they had anticipated, they moved to Los Angeles

to a small but sweet, nice adobe-style house in one of the canyons closest to Hollywood. I visited them a couple of times when I was in southern California, and they seemed to be adjusting to the change fairly seamlessly.

But R's screenwriting was not taking off as smoothly as he had hoped. As is so common in the glitzy but Kafkaesque labyrinth of movie business bureaucracy, scripts would get approved then rejected as personnel changed at this or that studio or production company, and there would be endless re-writes and promises, and just waiting and waiting for a green light, or after a while, any sort of response. One of the last times I saw him R was getting frustrated but was still sure his boat was delayed but not sunk, and in the meanwhile he was able to borrow money from relatives.

In the year or two after that I slowly lost touch with them, as other aspects of my life had changed, and I became much busier in New York and I was no longer going out to LA for other reasons, and had never been close enough to R and L to go there just to visit them. I then heard from a mutual friend who had remained in closer touch with them that their little girl, then perhaps around 5 or 6, had had a terrible accident and had lost most of two fingers when she stuck her hand in the wheatgrass juicer in their house. I called R a while after that to see how they were doing after the incident, and I was surprised by how radically transformed R seemed to be. He wasn't able to put any kind of positive spin on this incident and seemed really shaken, which was certainly understandable.

There was something about the symbolism of the terrible

injury caused by the wheatgrass juicer, one of the, to me, archetypal symbols of this couple's quest for perfection, discipline, and glowing health, that seemed ominous. I then really lost touch with them for a long stretch, but a couple of years later I got another report from the same mutual acquaintance, and the news was truly shocking.

Apparently L had been diagnosed with some sort of reproductive cancer, something that has tragically claimed the lives of quite a few women I have known, including several, sadly in their 30s and 40s. I don't know what her prognosis was, what her treatment choices were, whether she chose to deal with it using alternative approaches or conventional medicine. All I know is that in the last six months or so of her life she left R and her daughter and ran off to Hawaii with a new lover and then died some time after that. When I heard about it, it was already many months since it had all transpired. I called R, and he was holding it together, but this was no longer a man certain about anything, as he really didn't seem to be able to figure out why L had done what she did. It did seem truly out of character. Neither one of them ever seemed to me like the types to have affairs. They really had been a strong couple. Perhaps one of them had blamed the other for the wheatgrass juicer incident, but that's purely wild speculation on my part.

One thing occurred to me about L's behavior. It is of course possible that she just decided that since her life was ending she would have one last passionate love affair in a beautiful place. If that were the case I certainly wouldn't judge her for making such a choice. In fact, in my eyes, there's something admirable

about it on some level. But I just wonder if there weren't other elements to what she did. What if she wanted to free her husband and her daughter from a lifetime of worship of her memory? What if she somehow knew that R would have an easier time forming a new amorous bond with someone else if he felt betrayed by his wife and that her daughter would more easily accept a new mother figure? What if she didn't want to burden R with caring for her until her death, and especially didn't want her daughter to watch her die? Now one could argue that her behavior still caused enormous pain to her husband and child, and that's beyond dispute, but great pain was inherent in this situation no matter what.

I never spoke to her during that time, so I have no idea whether she thought of any of that or even harbored such notions unconsciously, but there's a part of me that thinks it's possible that L wasn't just being selfish, that in her final act she tried to combine a full embrace of life, of romantic, sensual fulfillment with an enormous emotional sacrifice—being willing to be viewed negatively for years by the one long faithful companion she'd had and by her own child, for what she may have felt was their good in the long run. One might argue that if that had been her logic, it is a twisted, self-serving train of thought, but I wouldn't be so harsh.

I really have no idea whether there's any truth to the scenario I just described, but I wouldn't be surprised if L tried in her own way to find as multi-faceted a solution as possible in a terrible situation, that she was still seeking what perfection she could with the hand she was dealt. Maybe that's just my own

romantic view of her, because though I was skeptical about their certitude and their quest for a certain sort of perfection, they did come as close as any two people I've met to realizing that ideal, in a "New Age" countercultural context anyway.

I long ago lost track of R and his daughter. I really hope he was able to put his life back together and to find fulfillment and success in some realm, and that she was able to thrive despite the traumas of her childhood.

This episode did permanently change me in one way: I no longer second-guess myself when it comes to my distrust of expressions of certainty in planning any human affairs. Now, if people describe their plans to me with an air of absolute confidence, no matter how charismatic and convincing they might seem, I no longer feel insecure about my skepticism. I have become far more confident about my belief in life's inherent uncertainty.

Animal Encounters

About the author

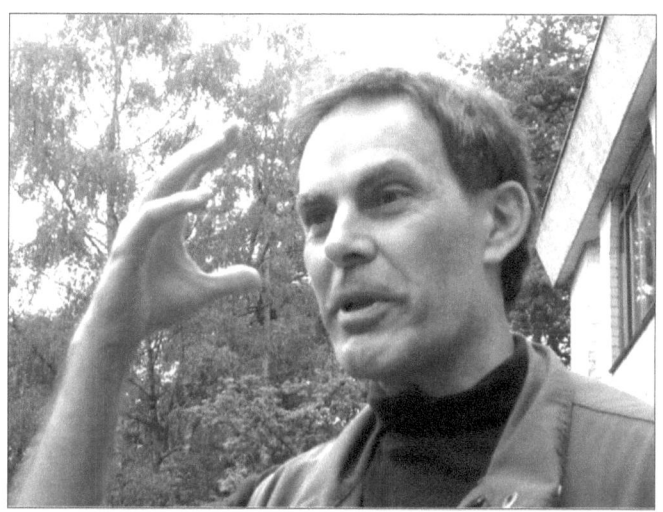

J.P. Harpignies is a Brooklyn, NY-based consultant, conference producer, copy editor and writer. He is the: author of several non-fiction books, including *Double Helix Hubris* (1997), *Political Ecosystems* (2004), and *Delusions of Normality* (2009); co-writer of *The Magic Carpet Ride* (2011); editor of the collection, *Visionary Plant Consciousness* (2007); and associate editor of the first two Bioneers books: *Ecological Medicine* and *Nature's Operating Instructions*. He has also been the associate producer of the Bioneers Conference (www.bioneers.org) since the early 1990s; co-founded the Eco-Metropolis Conference (2004/05); has served as a senior member of the Buckminster Fuller Challenge (www.bfi.org) review team since 2011; and was formerly a program director at the New York Open Center (in the early/mid 1990s). JP also taught t'ai chi chuan in Brooklyn for 25 years.

Animal Encounters

www.ingramcontent.com/pod-product-compliance
Lightning Source LLC
Chambersburg PA
CBHW031117080526
44587CB00011B/1009